HEALING

D1744702

9780434035007

HEALING

edited by
LORNA ST. AUBYN

foreword by
SIR GEORGE TREVELYAN

HEINEMANN : LONDON

William Heinemann Ltd
10 Upper Grosvenor Street,
London W1X 9PA
LONDON MELBOURNE TORONTO
JOHANNESBURG AUCKLAND

First published 1983

© Lorna St. Aubyn 1983

SBN 434 03500 9 cased
    434 03501 7 paper

Photoset by Wilmaset, Birkenhead, Merseyside
Printed and bound in Great Britain by
Biddles Limited, Guildford & King's Lynn

Foreword
by Sir George Trevelyan

The phrase 'holistic healing' seems to be coming into common parlance. 'Holism' is a wonderful word, of deep implications – the whole is holy, healing is 'wholing', the restoring of the part to harmony with the holy Whole. This gives a clue to the extraordinary step in consciousness now taking place. Through the last three centuries, acute self-consciousness has developed; rational, intellectual, separative, with its masculine drive to control and analyse, and to 'conquer nature' (a terrible phrase). Egoism has grown with its urge to satisfy desire and gain power, even by force and violence. The more sensitive, tender, gentle, feminine side of our nature has often been repressed, with the result that the organs of perception for the subtle, invisible, living world of being have atrophied and gone dormant. Spirit is denied and even God, the Divine Source, is thrown into doubt in our agnostic age. Man came to be seen as an accident of chance, natural selection in a nature wholly indifferent to him. We experience ourselves as separate beings against a world of things outside ourselves.

Thus a rational, mechanistic and materialistic world-view took possession of our thinking. The body was accepted essentially as a machine and treated accordingly. Medical science, despite its remarkable achievements, has lost the capacity really to think wholeness.

v

Now in our generation a turn-about is taking place in the centre of our consciousness. We strive to recover the vision of wholeness. Some of the leading scientists, through their own research and reasoning, are rediscovering the truths known to the mystics for centuries. It is seen once again that the universe is not a mechanism but an affair of mind; that the Divine Source has poured itself out into an ocean of life and thought and continually goes on doing so; that all manifest life works as an intricate Oneness, in unity though not uniformity; that mankind is integrally part of nature and is the crown of evolution; that in core and essence we are spiritual beings and that the immortal, imperishable droplet of divinity descends into the density of the material plane to undergo training in a physical body. This body is then seen truly as a temple for housing the spiritual entity. The Greeks carved over the portals of their temples for healing and initiation the affirmation – MAN KNOW THYSELF AND THOU SHALT KNOW THE UNIVERSE. This statement can mean but little to the materialist, mechanistic outlook. With the re-emergence of the spiritual, holistic world-view it makes profound sense. The Greeks also knew that knowledge and wisdom began with wonder. Look at your body anew as a temple and conceive that it is made not by chance natural selection but by Design, by thought and wisdom, and that in its immense subtlety and complexity it reflects the whole universe. The ancient 'Hermetic' wisdom knew that the Law of Correspondencies held good everywhere – as above so below; as in the macrocosm so in the microcosm. The microcosm of the body contains within it and its evolution all the secrets of the universe. Indeed spiritual science, knowing this great truth, has by intuitive study of the embryo and the processes of growth been able to unravel profound mysteries of the Earth itself through vast ranges of time. We learn now to see that the Earth is in a true sense a living organic creature, with its own breathing, blood-stream, sensitivity and thought, and that we humans, the crown of evolution, are cells of that great body, integrally part of the Whole. We are therefore stewards of the planet.

And look what in our avarice and ignorance we have done with our stewardship. We have polluted the planet, physically, morally and mentally. We have denied our own spiritual nature and the divinity of Life, and we now bid fair to destroy the wondrous web of harmonious life which surrounds the Earth. It is now touch and go whether we can survive as a race. In Buckminster Fuller's phrase: 'The world is now too dangerous for anything less than Utopia'. But in all the chaotic breakdown of our time, there rises a supreme hope that the holistic world-vision will bring together a new society – almost a new human species – grounded not in violence, aggression and competition, but in co-operation, sharing and service of the living Whole of which we are cells. With this world-view an alternative, and life-affirmative, life-style naturally emerges, since those touched by the new understanding are naturally drawn together to find each other and become focal points for the shaping of a new society.

The subject of this book – Healing – reflects this awakening consciousness. All aspects of the emerging, holistic vision open ways to therapies which relate afresh to wholeness. In their diversity they all inter-relate, the different techniques presenting aspects of the holistic pattern.

These have been called the Alternative or Complementary Therapies. Many people, dissatisfied with conventional allopathic medicine with its basic reliance on chemical drugs and surgery, are turning to Natural Therapy and the different aspects of Healing. This is not in any way to belittle the remarkable achievements of medical science. We must, however, recognize that consciousness itself is evolving and that a great step is now being taken from self-consciousness to cosmic consciousness. Once we grasp the concept of holism we must seek out ways to health which respect the oneness of all life. A true science of health is beginning to shape. Exploration is continually pressing forward into new fields of holistic knowledge, and its findings bring immense hope and encouragement. Even the horror of cancer is seen as the result of deviation from the Divine Law, and a restoring of harmony with this Law very frequently brings relief and restoration to health. For health is our birthright. The healing movement in its many aspects is directly placing responsibility for our health upon our own shoulders. We can do something about it and take the initiative. We have brought ill health upon ourselves by doing things which throw the body temple into disharmony. We can learn how, in our ignorance, we have been poisoning and damaging this miraculous and sensitive organism – and then learn how to stop doing those harmful things, thinking those negative thoughts or putting those life-killing toxic substances into ourselves. It is basic to health that we eat life-generating food, fresh and alive and much of it raw. Nature, living and active, knows how to heal if we give her the chance. The prospects ahead are bright indeed. We are on an adventure into a New Age, in which real health will be experienced as our true inheritance.

Lorna St. Aubyn and her co-authors give a most helpful introduction to this important field, clarifying different aspects of holistic healing. May this book be widely read and bring to many the joy of restoration to real health.

Sir George Trevelyan

The Authors

Lorna St. Aubyn was born in London in 1929 and spent much of her earlier life in the USA and on the Continent. She developed an interest in healing when her two children had grown up and left home; she now practises and teaches healing techniques.

The Reverend Gordon Barker was educated at Oundle School and served in the infantry during the Second World War, after which he entered the family timber business as a director. At the age of 40 he went to the Central College of the Anglican Communion at Canterbury where he trained for the priesthood of the Church of England. He spent ten years as a country parish priest but for some twelve years now has exercised a non-stipendiary ministry of counselling and healing, also teaching simple forms of relaxation and meditation.

Sylvia Johns was born in 1928 in the Gower Peninsula in South Wales. She was educated at University College, Swansea, and spent a number of years in retail management. In 1969 she joined the English Department of the Girls' Grammar School at Tonbridge in Kent and taught there until 1977. Since then she has been engaged in fund-raising for charity.

Dr David Smallbone MB, ChM, was born in Birmingham in 1938 and educated at Kings Norton Grammar School, Birmingham University and London colleges. He qualified as an MB in 1961 and as a homoeopath at the London Faculty of Homoeopathy in 1964. Since then he has been in practice in the Midlands and also teaches self-healing techniques.

Michael Wetzler BA (Cantab), MBBS, DCH, has a degree in Mathematics and Philosophy of Science from Cambridge; he decided to study Medicine after contact with various dedicated doctors including a homoeopath. He has maintained an interest in alternative healing practices throughout his studies, participating in the arrangement of lectures and explorations in various fields. He has undergone his own psychoanalysis and is trained in Transpersonal Psychology as a counsellor. His principal current activities are Paediatrics and Psychiatry in a medical context, and occasional workshops and lectures on Healing as practiced by Dr Brugh Joy, Doctor turned Healer, in the USA.

Acknowledgements

We would like to thank Brian Snellgrove for his permission to use the Kirlian photographs that appear in this book.

Contents

'It's a professional secret, but I'll tell you anyway. We doctors do nothing but aid and encourage the doctor within. All healing is self-healing.'

Albert Schweitzer

Introduction

During the past few years, there has been a strong revival of interest in healing. And like all subjects which receive sudden and immoderate publicity, it has been seriously misrepresented. Such patently impossible claims have been made on its behalf that many serious people have dismissed it without further exploration. Also, more destructively for the understanding and growth of healing, its over-enthusiastic supporters have created an unnecessarily deep divide between it and orthodox medicine.

This book will try to restore equilibrium to the picture by first of all defining healing and its many subdivisions, and then setting the twentieth century healing movement within the framework of world history so that it can be seen as a serious revival of knowledge from many different civilizations. Its third objective will be to give a sober assessment of the similarities and differences between orthodox medicine and healing so that we can see what their relationship could and should be.

We will also try to help, with practical advice, those who want to be given healing as well as those who may have discerned in themselves a potential for giving healing to others. We are moving into a new era where we shall be *forced* to make restitution for what we have in the past done to the earth and to ourselves. It is only through our willingness to receive and give healing, each to his full capacity, that we will be able to re-form our most basic relationship with the planet, with the animals, with our fellow-men and with ourselves. So the whole question of healing is central to the world situation. And because the need is so urgent, the intuitive, receptive qualities necessary to a healer are emerging in more and more people, so that eventually the logical scientific part of our mind, which is at work in orthodox medicine, will be completed by its counterpart in healing and the two branches of knowledge and wisdom will work together.

In defining the word healing, it seems best to divide it first of all into two main categories: healing where only hands are used, and healing where use is made of physical aids such as needles in acupuncture, a pendulum in radiesthesia, etc. As this book is mainly concerned with hand healing, we will not enter into great detail about therapies which are outside this category. Let us now further subdivide hand-healing to explain three terms which are often bewildering and misunderstood: faith healing, spiritual healing and spiritualist healing.

'Faith healing' is a rather misleading expression as it implies that faith in a particular creed is required in order to receive healing. Such an assumption so limits both the healer and the patient that this term would be better avoided unless specifically agreed upon.

The expression 'spiritual healing' is generally used when associating the phenomenon of healing with the Church. It presupposes that a Force greater than man created the world and can therefore heal what has gone wrong. Someone who calls himself a spiritual healer would almost certainly be assuming that man is essentially a spiritual being. It is not, however, necessary for a patient to espouse any formal religious teaching in order for his health to be improved or restored by a spiritual healer.

The term 'spiritualist healer' can create even more confusion and should be well understood because its basic premise is very specific and is not one that very many people accept. Spiritualist healers believe that their healing work is directed by discarnate spirits, often those who were once doctors. These 'Guides', having knowledge of the patient, can often diagnose and treat his illness through the healer.

It is because of the confusion so often arising from these three terms that we have agreed to use in this book the expression hand-healing when referring to healing that is given exclusively through the hands.

The possible sources from which healing derives is another subject which will be discussed. Whether said to be stemming from God or not, a limitless primal energy or Force appears to be at work within all things. It flows, more or less well, through our bodies and through all of nature. If either its entry or circulation becomes blocked, the organism will become unwell, and it is then the job of the healer to channel that force and restore its flow. The Kirlian photographs included in this book show the process at work.

Healing energy can also be drawn forth from the healer's own body, but unlike the primal force mentioned above, this source of energy is very limited. It is the energy that people use unconsciously when holding a patient's hand in hospital or hugging a sick child. Healing given in this way with love can be very effective, but as we will see later, it can also create difficulties and dangers if the giver is using his own energy instead of channelling primal energy. The donor can become very easily depleted, and if he does not know how to regain the energy needed for his own use, he will eventually become ill.

That these are in fact the only two potential sources of healing should be made quite clear at this point because much misunderstanding has been caused by misinterpretation of the role of discarnate entities or dead souls in Spiritualist healing. It is never their energy which is being used; they are simply acting, along with the healer, as intermediaries between the patient and the Life Force already mentioned.

To define the objective of healing is the other main

purpose of this book. This may at first sound ridiculous. Clearly good health must be its goal. But as the book progresses it will be seen that health and ill health are not such simple concepts as we had perhaps imagined. We are not just mechanical constructs, the parts of which can be restored or replaced as though we were a motor car. We are a Whole whose spirit, mind and body must all be functioning both well and in unison. We are also an integral part of the entire world. And unless we are fulfilling our role within our family and at work and as a citizen of the world, we will not be truly well. It is not fortuitous that this great renewal of interest in healing should coincide with the birth of Ecology as a vital new Science. Healing is not only for the individual, it is for our planet, because they are totally interdependent. We must learn, before it is too late, to restore order and balance within the microcosm of man so that order and balance be restored to the world.

1 Perspectives of Health, Healing and Wholeness

Since time immemorial man has been concerned both with maintaining his health and with returning it to those who have lost it. Many attempts have been made to define health: the modern definition used by the World Health Organization (WHO) can serve us as a starting point: 'Health is a state of complete physical, mental and social well-being, and not merely the absence of disease or infirmity . . .' It then goes on to state that '. . . the enjoyment of health is one of the fundamental rights of every human being without distinction of race, religion. political belief, economic or social condition.'

Over the years, health has been predominantly the province of trained medical practitioners, but many other groups of people, including social reformers, priest-healers, and currently 'alternative' practitioners, have also focussed their interest on health and disease.

In order to consider the practice of healing, it is important first to ask ourselves whether the above definition is adequate and fully acceptable. For those trained in medicine (the word derives from the Latin *medere*, to heal), the definition should include the emotional aspect of well-being which is increasingly accepted as a dimension of health. Although such an inclusion sets a high standard, it

1

is a vital one for the purpose of establishing a definition of health which encompasses the whole person.

Levels of Being

In further consideration of health and healing, and of why emotional well-being should be regarded as an essential factor of health, it is helpful to see ourselves as existing on various interwoven levels, none better nor worse, greater nor smaller than another, but each one representing a different element of our human-ness. Each level, by becoming imbalanced or diseased, can in some way influence the others.

The first and most obvious level is the material, physical one. Here we sense our bodies and their interaction with the environment as defined in the first part of WHO's statement. On the second level, the psychological one, the world consists essentially of our relationship with ourselves and with others. It includes the mental and emotional aspects of our nature and on a wider scale the social well-being referred to by WHO. A third level can be postulated: this is the area of the spirit and the metaphysical, where there is neither form nor substance, but which carries what Jung calls the archetypal, universal themes. We connect with this level through dreams and the more intuitive non-rational aspects of ourselves. One can also hypothesize that we are governed or guided by something within this metaphysical world – either consciously or unconsciously – but belief in such a hypothesis is not necessary in order for someone to receive healing successfully. A fourth level is recognized by many, although once again belief in it is by no means a prerequisite for healing: this is the world of the Divine – that which is imminent and transcendent, which contains us and is contained by us, and about which nothing can truly be said because it remains unknowable.

Healing may be taken simply to mean 'making whole'. So often we sense in ourselves, in our body, psyche or spirit, an incompleteness, an imbalance or a dis-ease (lack of

2

ease). Our search for integration or wholeness is the quest for a complete Healing.

However, the quest for health may express itself on *any* of the levels mentioned, and here one of the great divides appears between orthodox medicine and healing. In the former it is assumed that the first two levels exist – and it is now accepted that they frequently interact. In the latter it is axiomatic that all levels are inextricably linked and interwoven, whether this fact can be observed and understood or not.

By looking at each of the levels separately we can begin to observe the pain or imbalance that leads us to seek healing, and to examine broadly the different therapeutic approaches that can be applied at each level.

The Physical Level

Our physical bodies have been very carefully and accurately described in countless text-books of anatomy, physiology, biochemistry and immunology. Clinical observation and classification of disease have been refined into a precise science which is in a constant process of further compartmentalization and change. If we damage any part of ourselves through interaction with our environment, be it by 'accident' or through toxic substances, or by pathological process, we can suffer a wide spectrum of acute or chronic problems, reversible or irreversible conditions. In dealing with problems on this straightforward level, medicine in the last hundred years has made much progress. It has defined the obstacles to good health by classifying infections, toxic irritants, lack of vitamins or minerals, hormonal imbalances etc. We have also learned to provide physical conditions in which healing may take place, despite the fact that the ultimate control mechanisms for healing have not yet been thoroughly understood.

It would seem that the problem in physical healing is not so much how actively to heal damaged tissue, but how to facilitate a natural biological process by removing the obstacle standing between the patient and good health.

3

The fact of the matter is that, except in a minority of situations, the body contains within itself the ability to self-heal. This fact can be more easily understood if we consider the body cells at a simple structural level.

Cells are divided into three types: a) labile cells which continue to reproduce themselves throughout life, b) stable cells which normally do not multiply, but which may reproduce themselves when tissue is damaged, and c) permanent cells which cannot replicate after infancy. At a cellular level healing takes place through the regeneration of tissue by labile and stable cells. In a situation where permanent cells are damaged, restoration of an organ to its original form is not possible. After any damage to the body has occurred, each type of tissue, composed of a varying mixture of cells, start to heal in its own particular way.

Another vital function of the body which can also go awry is the maintenance of its internal environment. Multiple biochemical and biological mechanisms should maintain this self-regulation, or homeostasis, but if derangement occurs, how should these processes be returned to full function? The response to this question is similar to that given about the regeneration of tissue. Although part of the task may consist in adding or subtracting, either medically or surgically, some body substance or some synthetic chemical to aid the rebalancing process, the doctor's main concern is usually to create conditions in which disturbance is minimized, so that as much self-healing as possible can occur.

A third way in which the body copes with a threatening environment is to develop its own defence system. This consists of various attributes such as a relatively impermeable skin envelope, and such methods for ridding the body of noxious material as coughing, diarrhoea and vomiting. In addition, there exists in vertebrates a special defence system adapted to repel specific invaders. We develop what is termed 'acquired specific immunity' to foreign material through a process whereby specific cells multiply to bind and/or destroy the invaders. The study of Immunology is growing rapidly and is expected by the

4

medical world to yield much fruit in the years ahead. But despite the inherent need for the immune response, it must be remembered that it too can go wrong, either through an exaggerated reaction to foreign stimuli, or by reacting to parts of ourselves which are not foreign, thus creating a 'self-destruction' process. One of the main research areas of Immunology is how to activate the immune response when needed and to suppress it when excessive.

Medicine has learnt, through understanding the above aspects of the body's processes, to influence its structure and function. In order to do this, it may use no more than 'conservative management', leaving well alone, and allowing the body to heal itself as much as possible. This solution is more common now than it was at the beginning of the technological boom, when it was felt that all disease would ultimately yield to the weapons of science, (a view still widely held in many orthodox circles today). The alternative to 'leaving well alone' is the use of intervention such as surgery, radiation or drugs. Dietary management has also theoretically become an important part of the treatment of disease, although evidence for this is sadly lacking in most public clinics or hospitals. Other possible physical approaches to relieving suffering include physiotherapy, exercise and occupational therapy, each in itself a complete field of endeavour.

As many of their practitioners would agree, the above therapies are not in themselves totally physical. There are also others which form bridges between the worlds of the body and of the psyche. These we shall discuss later.

The Psychological Level

This brings us to consideration of the psychological world, which although it has gained in general understanding and appreciation in the last century is still often misunderstood and underestimated. If it can be seen as a broad and general realm of thinking, feeling and relating, rather than as the province of those who deal with the mentally or nervously deranged, then we shall see that the limitations sometimes

5

associated with the term psychological are more often the limitations of the people involved in applying its criteria rather than limitations of psychology itself. We shall be using the term here not in the specific and exclusive sense given to it by many philosophers, psychiatrists, analysts, novelists and others, but in a broader sense which includes everything which is neither purely physical nor spiritual – although it will be assumed, as stated before, that the three domains interrelate at all times. Our field of enquiry will encompass both the extremes of psychopathology, such as schizophrenia and overt psychoses, as well as the fluctuations of mood and mentation, both minor and severe, to which all of us are subject. It will also include the conditioning processes of our upbringing with all their helpful and detrimental influences.

There is a wide range of possible approaches to understanding the psyche and helping us attain some degree of psychological balance or wholeness. Each of us will be drawn to one particular approach by what appears to be chance, or else by a more conscious response from our own particular nature. But whichever way we choose, it will have one thing in common with most, if not all, of the others: the answer to the problem of wholeness, balance and integration lies ultimately within the individual. In this respect the psychological processes parallel the biological ones: both have the potential to regulate and heal themselves.

In the same way that the various methods cover a wide range of therapeutic possibilities, so do their aims lie on a wide spectrum. Some seek to restore the patient to his 'status quo ante' (or state of mind before his illness); others hope to leave him with a profound understanding of the roots and origins of his thinking and behaviour patterns. Many seek to help the individual release himself from those obstacles that are preventing the realization of his fullest potential. Therapies for healing of the psyche include both material and mental factors. Much psychiatry (from the Greek *iatros*, doctor, of the *psyche* or soul) uses drugs to effect the psychological through the physical, but there are

6

numerous other techniques in which the therapist functions principally as a mirror in which a patient/client can begin, often laboriously and painfully, to attain balance by seeing himself objectively.

The Spiritual Level

Let us turn now to the third level of our being, as postulated in our description of man as existing on three or even four different levels. The world of the spirit is a subject which is more nebulous and difficult to discuss for, in a sense, its area or existence could be considered to be beyond words. Yet most people would admit to its existence, even if only negatively, feeling that 'there *must* be' something beyond that which they can see and touch and feel. Taken more positively one could define it as that part of our Being which joins us to all other living creatures. It is our link with the earth and with the Universe, with the past and with the future. Yet unless one has been personally convinced of the reality of the spiritual world by the kind of subjective inner knowing which has been described by many people throughout history, either one is of necessity relegated to the realm of faith, which is becoming increasingly difficult for modern man who tends to view faith as intellectually suspect, or else one must achieve a state of open-mindedness, a suspension of prejudice. To admit to the possibility of a level existing not only beyond that of the everyday world but also beyond that of the unconscious – which for many people is the limit of what they can accept – often requires a great effort. If a temporary suspension of disbelief could be made, it might well be found rewarding to reconsider the whole matter consciously and willingly, detaching it from the rather limited and obsolete context in which most of us encase the concept of spirituality. If we can here define spirituality simply as that which is beyond form or substance, it is no longer necessary to place it within any doctrine or theology but only to accept that there is a world, as yet known only to a minority, beyond the five senses and the psyche.

7

Such an acceptance may well be the only means by which a healer's patient can actively contribute towards the process of his own healing. He need not, we re-emphasize, believe in or have expectations from any therapeutics mode in order to benefit from it. If he can make himself receptive and 'listen with his heart', using neither his emotions nor his intellect alone, but a combination of the two, he will put himself in the most favourable possible state for receiving whatever healing is being transmitted to him.

It is important to realize that there are many degrees of intent in healing, many different levels on which the healer can be working. The ultimate goal of healing is perceived in the alchemists' search for the universal medicine or elixir of life. This was said to exist 'if only it could be found or formed', and was supposed to be the agent through which man would attain eternal youth and immortality. For true disciples of Alchemy this immortality was seen as the spiritual and mysterious reunion of man with the One, the source of life, the first light from which creation flowed. By embracing all existence it becomes the completion of wholeness. This ultimate goal concerns us here mainly to show us the full spectrum of possible healing rather than to become part of our practical consideration, for, as has been noted elsewhere, many are called to such total union, but few are chosen.

Relationship between Healing and Man's Different Levels

Having moved along a set path describing man from his physical level to the spiritual one, let us now retrace our steps and discuss the relationship between Healing and each of these realms. Before doing so, however, it must be pointed out that the aim of healing is often not the same as that of most orthodox medicine. Healing seeks to allow or facilitate the expression of a person's greatest potential. It helps to achieve the maximum growth and understanding of a personal self within a greater whole. What could this mean to the patient? One essential characteristic of healing in its widest context is that it seldom conforms to our expectations; it could for instance include acceptance of pain and self-sacrifice. In this sense it may well not fulfill the tidy format of the WHO definition, or even contribute in part to it. We are conditioned since childhood to expect healing to manifest on the simple physical plane as a cessation of pain or a regeneration and repair of tissue, or as a restoration of function to a disrupted limb or organ. This, however, is not necessarily the case when health is considered from a wider viewpoint. History provides us with many examples of individuals who have been prepared to sacrifice their physical health or even their lives for issues they considered more important than life itself. Schweitzer, Ghandi, and Mother Theresa are three modern examples of this. By giving their lives to others even to the detriment of their physical health, they achieved a wholeness which is the exact opposite of recovery in the sense we normally understand it. It is a wholeness which can show itself at a time of great illness and pain, and of which death simply becomes a part rather than an ending. It is essentially an internal reorientation which allows us to accept and embrace our fate or destiny. It is a relinquishing of all the major and minor motivations that drive us, and it is trusting that this abandonment will allow a greater potential and wholeness to be expressed. In a sense this wholeness gives freedom from the limitations of the physical body rather than changing the limits themselves, although the latter may occur as a secondary effect. One of the main obstacles in the path of this process is fear; work towards freedom from fear is therefore a prime requisite on the road to wholeness.

Alice Bailey, in her book *Esoteric Healing*, suggests that the primary task of healing is to prepare us for our death. She sees death itself as 'the great restorative process'. By reconciling ourselves to our mortality we can more easily dis-identify the self from the body and re-identify with that aspect of ourselves that we have called spirit or soul.

The task of facing one's death has been used as an initiation rite in many cultures. In the modern Western world, the opposite attitude has prevailed for many years:

death has been a taboo subject, neither spoken of nor faced. Now a lifting of the taboo has begun but it is not yet a task which most of us can take on easily. It is said by several doctors who work with terminally ill children that it is they – not yet conditioned by our society's fears – who can often die most peacefully and gracefully.

Theories of Healing

At this point it would be useful to look at various theories of healing and see how, although they are differently expressed, each one allows for healing on all levels from the esoteric to the mundane.

The concept of energy is a common underlying feature of many explanations of healing. For the Newtonian physicist this idea presents difficulties, as energy is for him a very precise term. However since Einstein's theory of relativity, energy and matter have been recognized as interconvertible and as a result the term 'energy' may be used a little more loosely.

Let us then hypothesize the existence of an energy field around the human body – rather akin to an electromagnetic field. It would exist not only outside the body, it would be an integral part of it and display various degrees of subtlety and coarseness depending on its position. It would also interact with the body, possibly changing its organization, and could be in some way transmittable to other individuals and to the environment.

In Eastern religions there is an axiom arising out of the concept of energy which is formulated in the statement: 'Energy follows thought'. This may either be taken at face value in that thought precedes action and consequent expenditure of energy, or it may be understood at a more subtle level. The above-mentioned energy fields can be influenced by undirected, habitual or focused thought, whether these thoughts are constructive or destructive. The consequences of the thought on the energy field will then influence the physical body. In this way healing can take place through a healer holding in concentration an

10

image of his client pictured as whole. It is possible either to work to a specific end or simply to hold the intention that whatever is most wholly appropriate be allowed to occur within that individual.

Two other theories exist as to how healing works. The first has a religious basis and assumes that prayer is the vehicle for healing. This form of intercession is practised by priests or by certain lay parishioners either privately or during church services, more of which are now labelled Healing Services and declare their intent to heal through the Laying on of Hands rather than relying on group intention as is done when the 'Sick' are remembered by the Congregation.

The other theory, which I do not propose to discuss here, is that spirits or 'entities from another world' act through the healer, bestowing upon him knowledge which he could not normally possess.

In his book *Clairvoyant Reality*, Lawrence Le Shan explores paranormal experience. Within this domain he includes healing. In researching a number of people with reputations as healers, he has recorded the common denominators in their activity while healing, and eliminated the idiosyncratic or personal. Two types of processes emerge, whatever the theoretical system upon which the healer has based himself.

The first type corresponds to the open-ended approach mentioned above. It is achieved through an intense concentration on the essential unity between healer and client, who are seen as two persons in a universe infinitely larger than either of them. This profound shift in relationship with himself and the universe develops in the client a new existential position, creating what Le Shan describes as an 'ideal organismic situation'. In this situation the patient's abilities of self-repair and recuperation are activated to a degree far beyond the normal. There is however never any suggestion that the impossible could be possible. The permanent cells, which cannot replicate after infancy, are known to be unable to divide and cannot therefore help in the repair process. However, the other

11

two types of cell can be helped to speed up their multiplication, making apparently miraculous cures occur. It is the healer's capacity to link in, by intent, with the deepest element of 'being-ness' in his client, that facilitates, or even instigates, this repair process. Because this linking process is not recognized by Science and cannot be tested, acceptance of its existence is a jump which not everyone can yet make.

The second inner process reported by healers is focused rather than open-ended. Here the hands are used as the agents of healing, directing a flow of energy to the problem area. So sensitive do a healer's hands become that he perceives through them patterns of activity relayed to him as heat, tingling, pain or other signals which he learns to recognize and interpret. In this situation, some healers see themselves as originators of the healing energies, while others consider themselves channels for a universal energy which, by innate gift and training, they are able to tap.

An Eastern system based on the concept of energy is often used to explain healing. It postulates the existence of seven major energy centres, or *chakras*, in our bodies which constantly receive energy from a universal source and radiate it outwards more or less simultaneously, and more or less effectively, rather like an individual relay station acting for a universal radio-transmitter. Illness or disease are said to result from one of the following situations: a blockage in the receiving or radiating process; overstimulation of the receiving or radiating process; a blockage or overstimulation in a connection between two energy centres. Healing occurs when balance is restored to the individual chakras and free-flow is re-established between them.

The seven major centres, together with various minor centres (depending on the particular cosmology), are thought to include within them all the personal, social and universal aspects of man. Any one of these can be released to function more effectively as a result of the healer setting free these internal flows of energy. It is again a case of self-healing instigated by the healer's grace and practice but carried on by the patient's own energy system. The setting in motion of this process can again be seen as an open-ended or a focused act by the healer. Either he has tried to link the patient directly with the universal source of energy and left the details to be worked out according to universal will, or else he has by intent directed that energy through his hands to focus on one particular chakra.

The process of diagnosing disease, which is seen by most healers in terms of 'energy imbalance', is carried out by one or other of two processes similar to those used in healing. In the first instance an open, receptive attitude allows the healer to observe his own inner imagery and activity, and trust it as being a reflection of his client's. In order to do this he may or may not place himself in a trance-like state. Using the second technique he 'scans' his client's energy field receiving the diagnosis from the sensory messages of his hands.

Before attempting to explain this process in more generally acceptable terms, it is worth considering the behaviour of this 'energy' when used by groups rather than individuals. If one can accept that there is a healing force available to individuals who have learned to tap it, one can readily imagine that a group of like-minded people could tap an even larger force. This is the experience of many people working in the field of healing who maintain that the power of a focused group is often greater than the sum of its parts. It is as though each individual were contributing a unique and essential quality to the healing process, and that it is then the group rather than the individuals which acts as a channel for the healing force. This corresponds very closely to the Christian teaching in which each person is said to make up part of the mystical body of Christ (in this case, Christ as Healer). This concept of a group being used for good is more easily understand-able if we consider the more obvious and alas familiar sight of a group being used to cause riot and destruction. Very rarely would any one individual behave in such a way on his own but having become a cell of the group with its malific intention, he is expressing or channelling the group's type of energy rather than his own.

13

When the intention of a group is towards healing and wholeness, the potential for change is enormous. A Californian psychiatrist, Dr G. Jampolski, uses the power of the group in his work with terminally ill children. He finds that tremendous healing forces can be released within a group of children suffering from serious diseases. They can also be invoked in groups made up of these children's siblings and parents. Their diseases may or may not be remitted but if the children do die they have nearly always achieved a deep acceptance and peace through exploring together the calling-forth of love and healing. The enormous potential of groups seeking to bring harmony to the world can be a source of tremendous hope for a society which so often feels beleaguered by forces which it deems to be beyond its control.

To return to the potential effectiveness of individual action, I would like to give an example quoted by Brugh Joy in his book *Joy's Way*, because although it is not a direct example of healing, it is a very apposite example of the concept of interaction and unity which is such a fundamental tenet of healing. On a group of islands in the Indian Ocean, there live a species of monkey who had for many many years dug up their potatoes and eaten them unwashed. One day, however, a certain monkey went into the sea and washed his potato before eating it. His family followed suit, and gradually all the monkeys on his island did the same. But then, what could until now have been explained as a case of imitation, suddenly took on a new dimension: despite all lack of communication between the various islands, monkeys on nearby islands were performing the same washing ceremony. It was as if the collective focus of the monkeys had by distant induction transmitted the thought and action of potato-washing.

Although this story does not tell us anything about intentioned thought as used in healing, it does perhaps convey to us the instinctive equivalent of intentioned thought. On an animal level the monkeys' behaviour is a linking agent, as important in its way as the group behaviour mentioned above which can link consciousnesses and, by linking them, raise them. This very important principle of unity shows us that whatever is done by one monkey – or by implication one human being – influences all others. They also provide us with an insight into the phenomenon of simultaneity, the strange law that makes scientists all over the world 'discover' the same thing at the same time although apparently unconnected by any source of information. If we are so linked, then our responsibility for our own thought processes and their effects is enormous. It is clearly implied that each one of us can significantly contribute to the optimum development of the universe by working towards our personal wholeness and unity. And that when gathered together, even if only on an inner level, we as groups could work towards the unification and transformation of a divided world.

From the above discussion we see how deeply medicine/healing is connected to much wider issues. At a profound yet very simple level, the essential requirement for wholeness in individuals and the world may well be the evocation of a love so unconditional as to unite all people and heal all wounds. By unconditional must be understood two separate elements: the person emitting love must not choose or define or limit the recipients of his love; nor must he expect anything in return. His ability and determination to continue loving must not be contingent on the response or outcome of his loving. The sceptic may well reply that this is no valid solution. Yet it may be the keystone so long forgotten in the everyday practice and teaching of medicine, where although many individual practitioners show deeply loving natures, the model of the human being is often built up without consideration of this essential element. In the practice of any form of healing, unconditional loving is known to be an essential factor.

The 'Placebo' Effect

The successes of healers using the unconventional methods described above evoke strong reactions from orthodox medicine. They are often dismissed by doctors as

15

being the result of the 'placebo effect'. This is in fact trying to explain one unknown phenomenon, i.e. healing, by another phenomenon which is in itself not yet fully understood. The placebo effect is the outcome of giving patients a substance which although not chemically active, nevertheless produces an observable beneficial effect. This fortunate result is thought to be due to the attention bestowed upon the patient, or to the suggestion given him that a particular substance will help him. This effect can in fact be observed whenever any form of action is taken to remedy a particular problem; no physical substance is required.

The views expressed in an earlier paragraph could well explain the placebo effect far better than the placebo effect can explain what happens in healing. Attention is a basic aspect of caring and can therefore itself be a healing force. It is relevant to note that attention is also expressed in body language, and the hands are a vital part of the body's vocabulary. The healer's hands placed on a particular area may well be the means by which some change occurs in that area. That the placebo effect is due to suggestion is further explicable from the viewpoint mentioned earlier. If energy follows thought and suggestion is a form of thought, then benign results should follow a helpful suggestion.

Advances in Current Research

For scientists to dismiss as irrelevant the theories and practices of healing as outlined above would be to deny credit where results suggest that credit is due. But how can these scientists, to whom measurement and objective observation are essentials, judge healing fairly? Recently an increasing number of scientists of all disciplines have begun using their own equipment to assess what happens in both healers and their clients. Valerie Hunt, of the University of California, has demonstrated that high frequency electromagnetic waves are at times emitted from some people's bodies, and she has tried to correlate these frequencies with the colours seen by some healers/clairvoyants as 'auras'. In England Geoffrey Blundell and Maxwell Cade have developed a form of Electroencephalogram which they call 'The Mind Mirror', and which has shown that a healer's brain rhythms while healing can induce in the client a similar slow brain rhythm. Another research project which is currently attracting medical interest concerns body chemicals called encephalins. By assessing the changes in concentration and localization of these chemicals, it is hoped to understand how they create physio-chemical change and possibly affect consciousness. It is thought that they may be responsible for some of the effects of acupuncture, another form of healing also dependant on the concept of energy.

The Mechanistic Versus the Holistic Viewpoint

Because it is difficult for medical thinking to include reports of non-medical healing, the term 'spontaneous remission' is useful for explaining improvements which occur contrary to medical expectation. Whether or not a healer has seen the patient in the interim between the medical assessment and the 'spontaneous remission' is disregarded in medical reports. Another aspect of healing that must by definition be omitted from doctors' data is the concept of energy or spirit. As discussed earlier, the scientific definition of energy is strictly Newtonian, and the possible existence of energy or spirit as a unifying link of being-ness can be acceptable only to the religious believers within the medical profession. It is certainly not considered by the majority to be a necessary or effective factor in the treatment of a patient.

A medical pathologist from Holland, Dr De Vries, recently wrote a monograph entitled *The Redemption of the Intangible in Medicine*. In it he carefully builds up a model of our world and outlines man's place within it and within a more universal scheme. His plea is that we return to an acceptance of something intangible, not objectively observable, in order to be able to play our part in the universe. This intangible quality of which he speaks is closely akin to what we have earlier called spirit.

17

It may also express itself outwardly through what we have called energy. Taking this thought a step further, we might postulate that a medicine is merely accumulated energy focused into a small capsule or liquid. It is the sum total of all the caring, intention, research, scientific knowledge and also salesmanship of myriads of people that goes into the medical substance which, through the form the medicine gives to the intangible, exerts its therapeutic effect on the recipient.

If such a view is accepted, one must also accept that there are grave and inevitable consequences in dispensing a supposedly therapeutic agent which has been produced by such a mixture of 'energies'. There *must* be bad (toxic) effects along with the good ones. A completely different approach may well be needed if supposedly therapeutic action is not to bear these toxic side effects.

We have until now only considered the type of healing which uses no intermediary agent. Let us now briefly consider various other approaches to healing.

The Bach Remedies

Dr Edward Bach was a Harley Street physician who left his orthodox medical practice in the early 1920s to develop a system of healing now widely used as Bach Remedies. Based on 38 preparations of wild plants, bushes or trees which have been mixed with spring water and exposed to certain dosages of sun and air, the remedies are most efficacious in promoting health. Dr Bach's basic premise was that all illness, both physical and psychological, is caused by the inner forces of worry, anger, fear, depression etc. besetting the soul. As true healing can only come from within, his remedies were not designed to attack these forces, but rather to flood the soul with the appropriate 'goodness' which he felt to be inherent in each of his flower remedies.

His almost mystical approach, linking nature to the human individual and seeing peace of mind and inner happiness as the fundamental necessities for health, may

18

well be the most important lesson we should try to incorporate into our current medical practice. We mentioned earlier that healers aim to direct their inner energy flow correctly so as to catalyse a similar process in their clients. Dr Bach expressed this aim in different yet similar terms. He felt that the highest goal one can hope to achieve is to be at peace with oneself, because that peace will inevitably be transmitted to one's relations, friends, and clients, bringing them constant healing.

Bearing in mind our assertion that both the beneficial and toxic effects of a medicine may stem from the mixed multiple motivations entering its formulation, we could make a parallel statement about the Bach remedies: it may well be the purity of intent behind them which creates their effectiveness and eliminates the possibility of any side effects. However, this works both ways. Having been less used than more conventional drug treatment they are therefore more pure but conversely their accumulated energy and their consequent effectiveness must be far weaker. Nevertheless subtle results are achieved through them even though these may not be as obvious or measurable as science would wish.

Homoeopathy

Homoeopathy is very closely linked to healing and to Dr Bach's thinking by two common factors. It postulates the existence of energy as a positive factor and it asserts that 'Likes are cured by Likes'. Samuel Hahneman observed early in the 19th century that if a substance can cause certain disease manifestations, then a highly diluted form of that same substance will improve or cure those symptoms. The fascination of this theory in relation to our previous discussion lies in the fact that the remedies are often so diluted that no detectable trace of the original substance remains in the end-product. Our concept of intent must therefore be at work. The other now-familiar idea we must invoke to explain the phenomenon of homoeopathy is that of energy. If the efficacy of a remedy

19

increases through dilution, (a tenet of Homoeopathy so basic that this dilution process has been named 'potentizing' or making potent), we may surmise that the original substance must confer on its liquid vehicle, at a subatomic level, a configuration of energy which persists whether or not any of the substance remains after dilution. One can then hypothesize that it is the dilution process itself which acts as a transformer to increase the power of that configuration of energy. Every addition of liquid, and the associated shaking, are in a sense a reinforcement of intent for the effectiveness of the remedy. This accumulation of energy and intent are therefore increased rather than reduced by dilution. And so is the strength of the remedy.

Acupuncture

The theory and philosophy of acupuncture present us with yet another view of man. Again energy (*chi* in Chinese) is the underlying concept. In this case it is said to flow through the body along lines or meridians. This flow is regulated and governed by various organs, and if it becomes blocked or misdirected, health is impaired. The practise of acupuncture aims to restore the natural flow of this vital force. Years of study and observation are required in order to become an effective practitioner able to view the person as a whole, and able to help maintain or restore that wholeness. The Chinese approach to health is in some ways summarized by the fact that their practitioners are paid as long as their patient remains healthy; when he tips into a state of dis-ease, the acupuncturist receives nothing.

It is not my purpose to describe here all the many modes of therapy available, but it is worth mentioning those which, although working directly from the body, also act as bridge between it and the psyche and in so doing touch on spirit.

Osteopathy

Amongst these I include osteopathy, originated in 1874 by an American doctor, Andrew Still. Said to be in itself a complete science, it seeks to restore health by correcting structural derangements of skeletal parts. Osteopathic lesions are considered to be the significant factor in disease; these are treated by manipulations which, depending on the requirement of the patient, can be quite extreme or very subtle. The realignment of the skeletal system, especially the spine, can ease not only physical but also psychological complaints. Although the world of spirit does not play any direct part in osteopathic theory, it is felt by some of its practitioners that awareness of spirit may well enhance/influence the quality of healing that can be given.

Rolfing

Whereas osteopathy focuses its attention on the skeletal structure, Ida Rolfe, born in America earlier this century, focused hers on the realignment of connective tissue. She discovered that our patterns of behaviour and stress manifest in our connective tissue structure and that these can be realigned, through deep tissue massage, to allow emotional reintegration and physical health. It would appear from her teaching, however, that this form of therapeutic intervention is deeply effective only when a sense of the nebulous, intangible is allowed to participate in the healing.

The Alexander Technique

A further attempt to fulfill the human potential was explored by F. N. Alexander early this century. He was an actor who, having found that he was not functioning effectively, began observing in himself deeply ingrained patterns of movement and being. Through laborious self-discipline, he discovered a way of teaching himself and others how to re-establish effective functioning, principally through re-learning what we have forgotten while being 'brought up'. Alexander's method seeks freedom for the entire body structure which can then percolate into our psyche, bringing us to a greater sense of unity with the world in which we can then function more effectively.

Changing the Pattern

At the heart of all approaches to wholeness lies the search for inner freedom or release from suffering. The methods for attaining it vary, but it seems to be generally conceded that stultifying, over-established patterns of thought and function stand between us and this freedom which is really the basis of health. All therapies, ranging from the intangible approach of hand-healing to the refined and practical one of acupuncture, seek in some way or other to release the individual from cycles of thought and behaviour which have locked him into suffering. In this sense healing and release could almost be considered synonymous.

In some esoteric systems these deleterious cycles of thought and behaviour are said to extend over more than one lifetime. In systems based on one life only, the cycles are accepted as being established by heredity and early life experiences. Maladapted response to further experiences and the unconscious attracting to oneself of more damaging situations reinforce and perpetuate these cycles, limiting the fulfillment of the individual's potential.

Whatever the theoretical system whereby release is sought, the process required can always be seen as a path of transformation. As the caterpillar metamorphoses into a butterfly, so the individual who is ensconced in his or her pain can be released to a higher and fuller state of living and being by a process which is inherent in human nature. For various reasons, but principally fear of the unknown (of which death is the epitome), we limit ourselves to the caterpillar stage. Healing tries to help us become as complete and beautiful a butterfly as we can be.

Basic Questions

In discussing healing, it has been impossible to avoid asking the essential questions about life: Who are we? What are we? Where have we come from and where are we going? Possibly the greatest criticism to be levelled at conventional medicine is that while it has so brilliantly developed twentieth century technology, it has almost entirely lost sight of these questions, and makes decisions on life and death issues without reference to the fundamentals. This healing does not do. However much one can accuse some non-orthodox therapies of certain imprecisions and nonsense, they do at least provide belief systems attempting to explain these deeper issues. These we would do well to study with some care, for we are living in an era when the definition of our attitudes and goals is not only vital for our growth and evolution but for our very existence.

The Hologram Analogy

One other concept demands mention because it too is comprehensive enough to encompass fundamental questions. Holography is a special kind of photography; the hologram is the image which it forms. Its very specific and exciting property is that if you divide up the photographic plate, its parts do not contain *portions* of the whole – they each contain the entire image, although with loss of clarity. This idea inherent in the hologram has been used in the study of the brain, producing the hypothesis that each brain cell actually contains within itself all possible information and functions. But existing on its own, its information and potential for function are blurred and therefore limited. Joseph Chilton Pearce in his book *The Magical Child* further discusses the possibility that a single cell encompasses the working of the entire brain, and that the brain could well be a hologram of the planet earth. What would this imply? If each brain is a blurred, so far unclarified image of the whole earth, so may every part of the earth be a holographic picture of a far greater universal order. Mr Pearce quotes William Blake's poetic and mystical vision of 'The world in a grain of sand'. Could we then assume that each of us already has access to the entire

23

collective knowledge of the human race – past, present and future?

In order for the hologram concept to be helpful in our discussion on healing, we must conceive it possible that a healer can redeem the wholeness of his client which he has recognized as part of his own hologram. In the same way that it requires a particular quality of vision to perceive the world in a grain of sand, so it requires the gift and training of a healer to tune into himself and know his client as a whole. It requires a further act of imagination and spiritual giving in order for him to give his client back to himself, thus enabling him to take the next step along his path.

The hologram idea also assumes the total interconnectedness of all life. If a healer is able to tune into his own hologram, this facilitates or catalyzes the same process in his client. Evolution may then be seen as a process of clarification of the hologram. Our task is the discovery of the whole picture and purpose of mankind. Having learned from the hologram that the part not only reflects the whole, but also *is* the whole, we seek our own wholeness, because the wholeness of one person is vital in lifting the quality of the whole human race. For those who work as healers or physicians this process is even more vital for we are so closely and deeply affecting others. The universal directive 'Know thyself' can be seen as a command to make conscious our hologram; it may also be regarded as the eventual goal of healing.

Choosing a Therapy

What then should we do when disease requires us to pay attention to our state of body and mind? The first answer which occurs to us is probably a visit to our GP. If we are fortunate he will have enough time and the prized quality of being an attentive listener so that through compassion and wisdom and the aid of a well-tried remedy, he may help us gain sufficient insight to shift our actions or attitudes so that the pain is relieved or assuaged. If the problem is more complicated and the GP refers us to hospital, we will be faced with a battery of tests. Now there will be the luck of the draw as to whether the physician we see is understanding or sharp, tells us the diagnosis or is overworked and rude. As we get drawn further into the medical system we may feel lost and rather alarmed, stuck with a diagnostic label and a programme of treatment but rarely with any information or insight into our condition. There will almost certainly be no suggestion that we can participate in our own recovery. The idea that pain is a signpost towards wholeness and self-knowledge will seem laughable in the hospital environment.

The chances of being disappointed by our treatment are high. The possible causes for this disappointment are many, but they will probably centre around a feeling that we have not been treated as an individual and that our underlying problems have not been dealt with, either because of the doctor's lack of interest or our own reluctance to confront deeper issues unless given some active encouragement. That many of these criticisms do not apply in private practice, where time and attention are given in exchange for money, explains the current boom in private medicine.

But even private medicine is sadly lacking once we seek to learn from pain and imbalance rather than to suppress and disregard them. Where then shall we seek? How shall we choose amongst the many possibilities mentioned in this chapter and any others that we may have come across? The answer is not simple. We must make an act of faith either to accept the recommendation of a friend or to trust our own intuition. If you have been alerted to a preference within yourself for one form of healing or another and have sought advice from its professional body, then the only thing required of you is a willingness to listen and watch objectively. This suspension of disbelief in the process you have chosen is not blind acceptance but an open-minded, exploratory outlook.

W. R. Inge's statement in his book *Christian Mysticism* provides a good touchstone as to whether or not a particular approach is helpful to you:

'One test is infallible. Whatever view of reality deepens our sense of the tremendous issues of life in the world wherein we move, is for us nearer the truth than any view which diminishes that sense.'

So search until you find that sense of expansion rather than constriction. It exists for you, although it may not do so with the first practitioner or healing method that you try. And be prepared to give time and effort to your learning, for the deeper healing of which we have spoken will come only with time and effort.

In the field of healing there can again be disappointments, but quite different ones from those experienced through orthodox medicine. Be sure that you have understood the limitations of the therapy you choose before embarking on any treatment, because all methods do have limitations.

The greatest potential source of disappointment is certainly the healer himself. As he is not able to rely on external aids to the same degree as an orthodox doctor, his quality as a person is of prime importance. The maturity and fulfillment of his own life will in great part determine his ability to help a patient. Obviously knowledge and experience are important in a therapist but as we quoted Dr Bach 'The greatest gift a healer can give to his client is to be at peace himself.' There are of course grades of this peace, for it is not given to many to reach 'the peace that passeth understanding', as spoken of in the New Testament. But a healer who uses himself as an instrument should at least be on the path towards this peace and wholeness, possessing a high degree of integrity towards himself and his practice. To know this about a person is not always easy: the only reliable safeguards are trust in the mode of referral and trust in one's own intuition.

The third, extremely important, possible source of disappointment lies in the client himself. In healing, success or failure depend enormously on the patient since it is axiomatic that he is participating in his own healing rather than being acted upon. His expectations and attitude of mind when consulting a healer are then almost as important as the healer's abilities. He must shift from a state of passivity to a state of receptivity, that is to say a state in which he too is contributing to his healing by becoming aware of and able to use the peace and balance being offered to him. If his process of self-discovery is to be fruitful, he must allow the patterns of his past to dissolve in order that new more creative patterns can form. If he is not able to do this, it may be necessary for him to plod along the same road of suffering until such time as he is truly ready to change direction and begin transforming. There are undoubtedly stages of one's life where something in one's nature still *needs* the suffering one is going through. At these times there is nothing a healer can, or indeed should, do to alleviate the suffering, whether it be physical or psychological. His gift to the patient at this point should be one that has no immediate visible effect but is working on the patient at a deeper level to give him the insight and courage necessary for the next step forward.

Conclusion

People often ask whether everyone can become a healer. Returning to our hologram: if each of us contains within himself a picture of the entire universe, we can all become healers by clarifying that part of ourselves which already has the power to heal. The same would be true for becoming doctors, musicians, biologists and practitioners of every art and science. But if all of us were to become practising healers, all other aspects of humanity would lack clarification. And as our evolutionary process is to make clear the whole scheme of the universe, and as we have not yet reached that state of evolution when we have free access to all aspects of the hologram, we would do well at the moment to confine ourselves to the task of clarifying a specific aspect of that picture. It is for us to find what that specific task is, thereby working towards our own wholeness and helping to catalyse the process in others. The answer then to the question of whether we could all

27

become healers is simply yes. However, that is not what we are all called to do. The practice of healing is only one small facet of Healing when taken to mean the path towards wholeness.

Looking back at the WHO definition of health, it seems that we do not quarrel with it. But we do feel that it expresses only one aspect of our humanity. The hologram or universal picture could, in a way, not be complete without disease or the so-called negative forces in our world. So has our exclusive emphasis on health been wrong? In shifting to the idea of wholeness, should we not include, transcend and become at peace with the basic opposites of good and bad, health and disease? In whatever way we choose to work, we can comfort ourselves with a quotation from 'The Ethics of the Fathers' which is part of the Jewish daily prayer book: 'You are not called upon to complete the work, yet you are not free to evade it.'

2 Disease: Its Origin and Treatment

In the preceding chapter we have been given certain definitions of health techniques seen from the point of view of a doctor who has explored and participated in both the orthodox and alternative worlds of healing. The following chapter is also written by a medically trained man, who is in addition a homeopath; he will again attempt to define health and healing techniques, but will do so from a different standpoint, thereby giving the reader a chance to compare two contrasting, though not contradictory, views of this most complex subject.

Definition

In order to determine what is normal health and how it is maintained, it is essential to have some working definition of *life*. Such a definition could be: that state in which the soul has become manifest in the dense matter of the present world. It would appear, certainly from a reincarnationist point of view, and probably from most others, that this is a temporary affair. Taken at its bluntest, any organism that is born, is born to die. Its time span obviously varies with each species, but all except the very simple organisms have a definite life expectancy. The amoeba, as such an example,

29

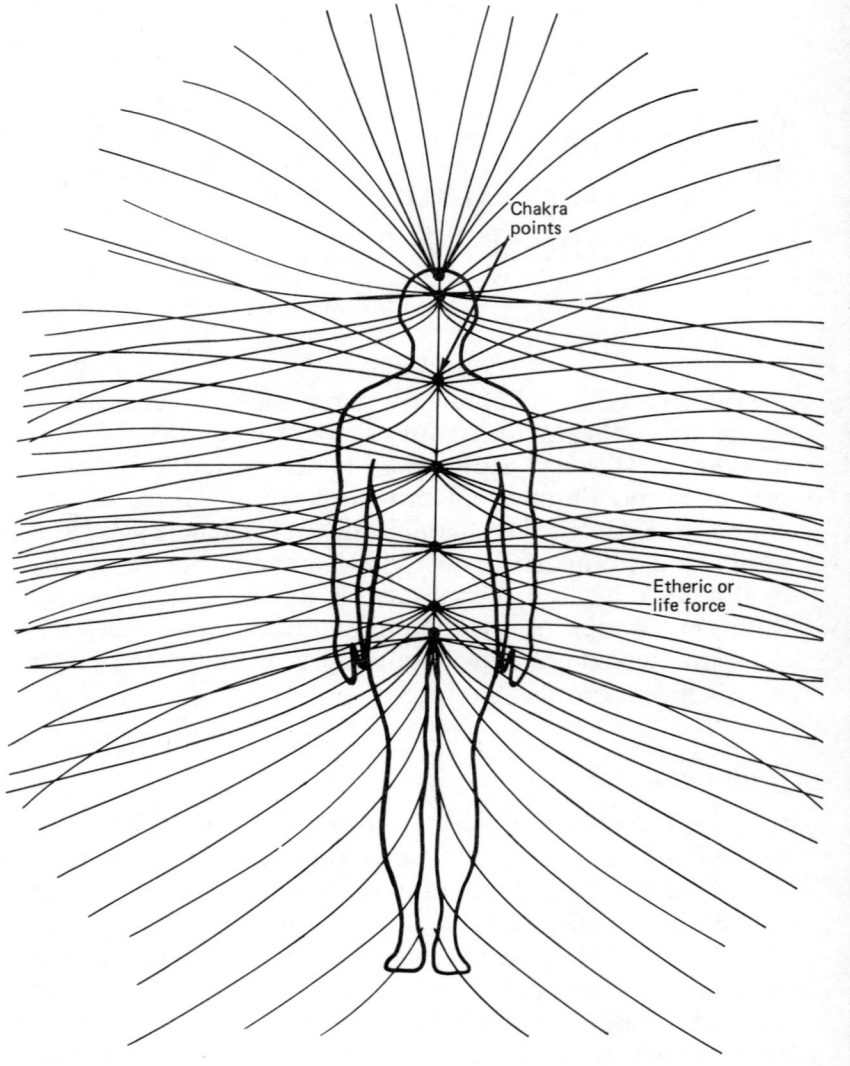

Chakra
points

Etheric or
life force

Figure 1

30

can rarely, if ever, be said to die: it merely divides and forms two amoebae, only dying if eaten or destroyed by artificial circumstances.

Any organism is in good health if it is able to continue living without outside interference and adjustment, while still persuing the functions for which it incarnated. How is this achieved? Perhaps Figure 1 may help us to understand this process.

The Etheric force, or Life Force, shown in Figure 1 maintains the organism's health. This energy, which enters the body at certain well-defined points known as *chakras*, binds and interpenetrates all matter, sustaining its form. Because of this sustaining effect, the Life Force promotes a state of well-being and creates what we call normality. If deprived of it, matter returns to its disordered state: chaos, from whence decomposition and disintegration. The health of the organism is dependant upon the Life Force not only being maintained but remaining in balance. Disruption may occur in many ways, either through the warping or disturbance of the Life Force itself, or through events occurring within the organism which produce an abnormal state of functioning. There may also be disruption of the interface or boundary area between the Life Force and the organism, that is to say at the chakra points. The main chakras are situated in a human being along the spine and are the points at which the relatively raw, ill-defined energy of the Life Force is refined for use by the organism. In mammals the chakras appear to distribute energy via various meridia and through conversion by the endocrine glands. They probably also work through other more subtle systems of which we are only just becoming dimly aware.

There are other spheres of action within us that can affect our well-being. Any aberration occurring in any of these, including the environment, is likely to have a disorganizing effect on the organism as a whole and thus lead to disease.

The terms used in Figure 2 should be understood as follows:

31

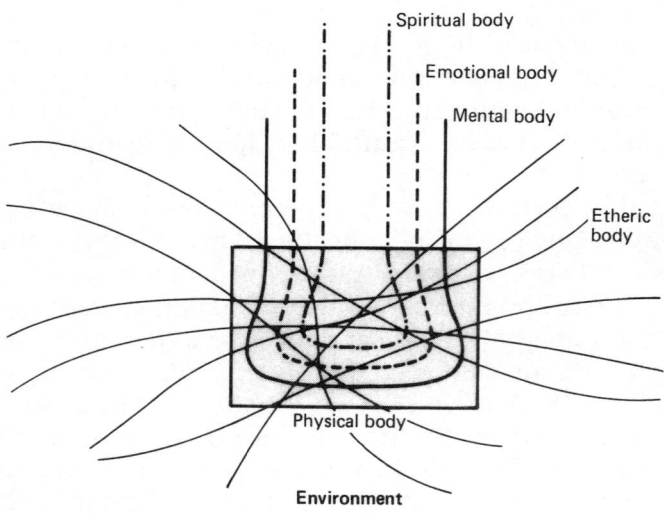

Figure 2

The physical body is that part of man which manifests in matter.

The etheric body allows the soul of man to create that material form and hold it together.

Through the emotional body the soul experiences the physical state.

The spiritual body induces the soul into incarnation and is its link with Primal Energy, the Creative Principle or God – call it what you will.

The sum of these parts constitutes the individual within his environment, both seen and unseen.

Traditionally disease is seen as the process of degeneration that leads to death. This appears to me a very short-sighted view, as the ultimate product of life must be death, (and we must therefore inevitably all become diseased). It is at this crucial point that we have to decide what our purpose is. If life is merely a chance happening and we exist

32

just because we are here, then the orthodox approach to disease is adequate. If, however, we see a reason for life, be it ever so humble, then the traditional approach, that is merely to prevent death for as long as possible, is totally inadequate. Life is an experience. We experience things in order to learn and to appreciate. Life is therefore a learning process. And learning processes only exist in order that we benefit from them. If death ends all, what benefit can we have derived from our experiences? Thus the prevention of death at all costs becomes meaningless, although it is at times vitally important to save life. Health then takes on a different significance more in line with the non-orthodox healing approaches. Thus I return to my original definition of health: good health is that state in which an organism is able to live and experience, without outside interference or adjustment, while still pursuing the functions for which it was incarnated.

As we have hinted, the maintenance of health is promoted by balance within the organism at all its various levels of existence. It must also be in balance and harmony with its environment and all its various ramifications. This state is the norm. Disease is therefore abnormal and is created by some action on behalf of the organism or the environment or the interaction between the two. Vigilance and acceptance become then our two main allies in the natural promotion of normal good health. These functions are usually carried on by the organism without too much stress or even recognition of their activity. It is only when a force or pressure is exerted upon some aspect of the organism, and the effect goes by unrecognized, that ill-health or disease ensue.

Disorganization

What is it that goes wrong within the living organism to produce disease? First of all let us define disease as a process of disorganization, occurring within an otherwise functioning organism, whose effect is to reduce that system to chaos.

It is often at this juncture that the viewpoint of orthodox medicine differs from that of other therapies. Orthodoxy sees most disease as being basically invasive, that is, occurring as a result of effects from external stimuli such as bacteria, toxic materials, other peoples' actions etc. The alternative therapies and the ancient forms of treatment, while accepting that external stimuli are often the agents of the disease, will on the whole maintain that the basic causes of it lie within the organism itself. It is spiritual or internal conflicts that create the initial disorganization. It must be said in all fairness that many doctors privately share this view, although it does not enter in to the scheme of 'scientific' orthodox medical practice. So where does the real cause of disease lie? I believe that both the above statements are true, but that by far the most powerful factors stem, at least initially, from within the organism itself. The environment usually only provides the 'final straw that breaks the camel's back'.

As we have seen, an individual is a complex inter-reacting collection of parts, living in an environment more or less congenial to him. For all practical purposes, this environment must be regarded as a 'part' of the individual, for without it he would have no physical existence. As well as these interacting parts, other individuals and their own 'parts' affect him. In a state of normal health there is balance between all these elements. But if you produce an abnormal state in one part, or prevent the balance between two parts, the whole organism can be upset and start producing disease.

Obviously in the initial stage of such a process, the imbalance is fairly simple. The direct action of one part upon another affects only the individual. Very soon, however, the situation becomes quite complex. If, for instance, the initial imbalance has occurred in the Emotional body, it not only directly effects the individual but also has an indirect action through the spiritual and physical bodies, and then goes on to effect the Environment. From there it begins causing trouble to other individuals, with resultant feedback and yet further

34

complications. Very soon the original cause for the eventual disease has become so lost in the complex interactions and feedbacks that it is almost impossible to discover.

Provided that disease conditions are simple and perceived early in their course we now have a basis for classifying them:

1 Internal causes
   a) Imbalances primarily affecting the various parts of the individual
   b) Imbalances primarily affecting the balancing powers between the various parts of man.
2 External causes
   a) Imbalances in an individual's environment
   b) Imbalances between individuals

It is rare however that we have only one specific cause falling into only one of the above subgroups. This is because other interactions have occurred by the time imbalance is detected. So the issue is nearly always further complicated by the fact that it is effectively one or more factors which may be the prime cause at any given time.

This does not quite answer our original question: 'What goes wrong to produce disease . . . ?' To answer this we must again assume some model of normality. For the sake of simplicity let us construct an individual of just two bodies: the Mental and Physical. In normal health these bodies are in balance, meaning that any bias appearing in one is counteracted by the other, rather like the pendulum on a clock. This is not a static situation but a dynamic one. First the pendulum swings one way, then the other, but each swing is roughly equal to its opposite. So with our two bodies; first the Mental Body energy predominates, then the Physical, and provided that these two energies are reasonably equal, balance and health reign. But supposing we place our finger in the arc of the pendulum, that is to say introduce a negating energy. Eventually we will upset the rhythm of the pendulum, thus effecting the clock mechanism, either slowing it down or stopping it altogether. So with our two bodies. Prevent equilibration between them and unbalance occurs; the whole individual is slowed down, cannot cope, and eventually grinds to a halt.

This is not, however, the entire picture. There is yet another process that can occur through a different agent. If we apply force to one body only (push the pendulum only from one side), we introduce a positive unbalancing force as opposed to the negating one previously used. By forcing the Physical Body, in this case, to accept more than its pressure of energy, we will cause disease. But more subtly and significantly we will often create a condition where the Physical Body pours its extra stress on to one of the other bodies (Mental or Spiritual), on to the environment, or on to other individuals. It must offload the system or collapse. There is another danger inherent in such a situation. If the positive disturbing force is removed from the physical body after this surplus energy has been offloaded to other sites, the system will go into overdrive in the other direction, straining the Mental Body and causing a whole new set of problems.

Rarely does this positive pressure-load produce death, in the same way that a simple interference with the pendulum rarely stops the clock. But it does tend to produce the most complex problems. And unfortunately the process can be taking place for some time before it is even noticed, thus increasing the likelihood of ever more complex interactions. The former example, however, the negating force, does often produce death in the individual by sapping all energy from his system.

What examples can be given of these two interfering forces – the negative and the positive? Bearing in mind that most diseases are composite in origin, we can only speak in general terms; illnesses such as cancer, coronary thromboses and endogenous depression are negative-reacting diseases, while such things as acute infections, injury and anxiety states, are positive-reacting. Obviously we must again consider the Environment to be another Body of the individual, so that factors affecting the Environment will produce in the individual reactions as

36

marked as those affecting his physical, psychological or spiritual Bodies (see Figure 3).

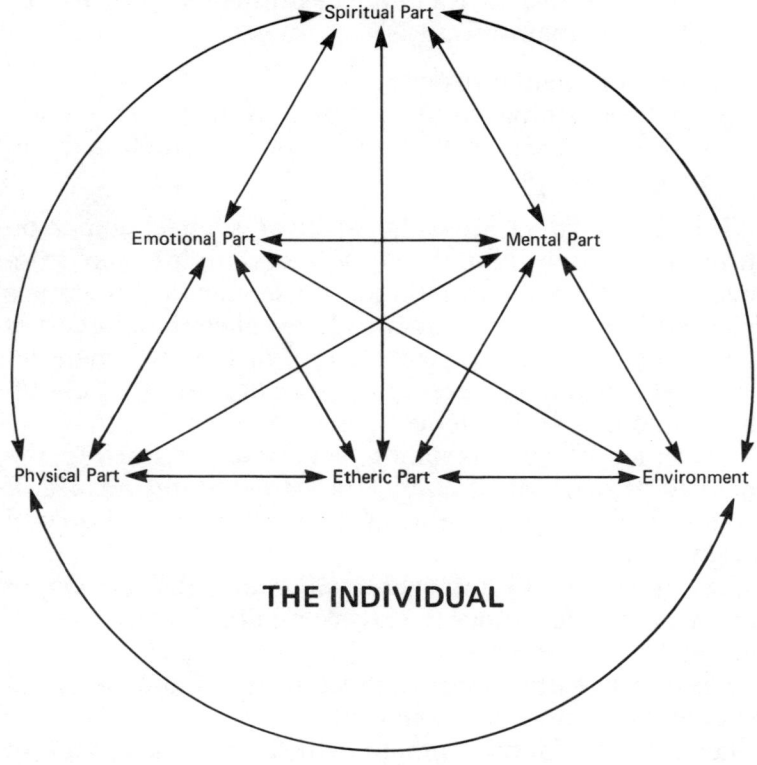

Figure 3

Prevention

The next obvious question we must consider is prevention. How do we stop these disease processes from occurring? The simple answer is, we don't, we can't. They are an inherent form of life experience. They are very necessary to the well-being of our whole organism. They force the individual to make adjustments, to react to living conditions. In the majority of cases they are the very essence of life. They are the tutor within the system, and they stimulate necessary changes in order that the organism should not become stagnant.

Having said this I do not mean that we must simply accept disease and do nothing. Certain causes of disease are man-made and can therefore be un-made. These factors fall into three main groups:

(a) Environmental toxicity
(b) Self-poisoning events inflicted on the physical body
(c) Self-inflicted events imposed on the emotional and mental bodies.

The first two groups almost always effect a person through his Environmental Body. As examples of environmental toxicity we can mention: toxic chemical materials released into the environment; chemical contamination of foodstuffs; and the removal from the environment of essential chemicals, resulting in such things as O_2 deprivation, iron deficiency, etc.

Examples of self-poisoning events are: smoking; the overuse of drugs in therapy, the overuse and misuse of chemicals for promoting growth in the plant and animal kingdoms.

Examples of self-inflicted events are the effects of unreasonable fear and the over-emotional responses of people to each other.

The effective prevention of these groups of problems will be dealt with more fully later on.

Let us return for the moment to the more general topic of prevention. As we have said, many of the seeds of disease are essential to the individual in order to help him become a complete person. But if allowed to develop to excess, unchecked and unrecognized, they will often lead to a destructive manifestation of disease. It is at this stage that prevention can intervene. But this is only possible if we are aware of the danger signals for which we should be watching. How do we know when some stimulus is reaching a state of over-stimulation? How do we recognize that something in us which has until now been creative is becoming potentially lethal to us? We must *know* ourselves. Awareness of ourselves and of our environment is essential to our well-being. Time and time again it is the deciding factor between illness and good health. We must learn to listen to what our various bodies are communicating to us. We have an inherent ability to do so, but often we ignore those still, small voices telling us that our body needs care; it is inconvenient or tiresome to listen and we crash on with our lives regardless.

But increasingly people are realizing that this is not a sensible pattern. How then are we to develop this awareness? I believe that it is done by learning to enjoy life. Awareness automatically follows joy. More formally, some form of meditation also greatly enhances awareness, both of ourselves and of our environment. Conversely bigotry and short-sightedness destroy it.

From the point of view of our health, awareness must include classification of what is normal and abnormal for us as individuals; acceptance of what is right for us; and vigilance at all times. Because we are all intimately and intricately intermeshed, our awareness must then grow to extend beyond our own state to that of others and to the environment. Disease does not only occur in individuals, it occurs in groups, in societies and in civilizations, and basically it has similar roots and causes whatever the circumstances in which it manifests.

Another aspect of prevention is that of *integration*. We should all be working at integrating, and thus balancing, all our various bodies and their interactions on each other. This again applies on the grander scale; our individual selves should be integrating with other individuals, other societies and the environment, so that in some small way we would be preventing the increasing malaise of our world. This brings us back to the idea of wholeness. When wholeness is splintered, disease can introduce itself.

The third aspect of prevention in this sphere is *correction*. Here again awareness plays a major role as this entails adjusting ourselves and our reactions while the imbalances are still minor and have not had time to become heavy issues with widespread ramifications.

All these three forms of prevention are inter-reliant. One is of little use without the others. We need awareness,

39

integration and correction in balanced proportions, complementing each other's functions.

Prevention of disease is then a complex, long-term pursuit. It must be seen as a continuous ongoing process, containing within itself periods of short-term corrective therapy. The whole organism/environment must at all times be considered in the widest sense to include the effects upon the individual of spiritual, emotional and mental factors, as well as the effects of wrong thinking and of the interaction between individuals. Never should one be waiting for disharmony to manifest before acting.

Here again orthodox medicine often differs from the complementary therapies. The orthodox approach is to wait until symptoms have appeared, then to treat the patient's specific condition regardless of occurrences in other parts of the organism. Little account is taken of future events. Occasionally physicians act as healers, viewing the overall person and trying to prevent rather than waiting for symptoms. Such people, until now, have usually been dismissed as unscientific – but times are changing.

Reversal

The next question we must answer is how to reverse this process of disease once it has occurred. The orthodox medical approach, considering man as the sum of his parts, treats most conditions as if they were isolated mechanical events. An appendicitis is dealt with by cutting out the 'offending' appendix; heart failure is treated by medicinally boosting or supporting the ailing heart, and so on. I do not believe that these methods are wrong, and I do believe that they are very often necessary in order to save life, but I also believe that they are not the *complete* answer. If the process of healing stops at removing the appendix or supporting the heart, then the root cause of the trouble will have been missed, and it is more than likely that some other manifestation of the dis-eased individual will appear. We must be failing in our complete duty as healers if we merely prevent the body from reacting by removing the symptoms. If the organism as a whole has given us an indication, more or less dramatically, that there is some basic problem to be corrected, we must listen to its plea.

Let us take as an example of the reversionary process an individual in whom the basic interference has been through some disturbance in the Spiritual Body. This upset via the Spiritual Body would almost immediately start having minor effects upon his other constituent parts, i.e. his Emotional, Mental and Physical Bodies and the Environment. Unless the original disturbance is corrected, several things could now happen. First of all a secondary attack might develop more powerfully than the first through one or more of the *other* parts of the individual. It is often at this point only that this disease process becomes overtly apparent; and because it has already become more complex it is then often incorrectly diagnosed. Because the fault is thought to lie in one of the bodies that has been *effected* by the disease rather than *causing* it, the wrong treatment is given.

Another difficulty that could arise in our example is that the Spiritual cause be perceived, but too late, and then be inadequately treated. Because of this inadequacy, its effect on the Emotional Body would still be felt by the individual. At the same time the Emotional Body would by now ostensibly have assumed the role of prime causal factor. But by the time it was being treated, it would have handed over the leading disturbing role to some other part of the patient, so that we end up in this case with a continuous need for therapy, pursuing all the different systems, but always remaining one step behind the disease process. Such a disaster unfortunately occurs commonly when the organism is not viewed as a whole. Inadequate treatment is in a sense almost more dangerous than none because of the complicated and misleading evidence it produces which confounds further treatment. In an example such as ours, we would have to deal fully with the patient's spiritual and emotional disease processes, and also look for the possible ramifications effecting all his other systems. Without such thoroughness we would run the risk of leaving behind the

41

germ of a future disease process, or fertile ground in which it could grow.

We must next consider the available therapies in the same light as we have considered the human individual: that is to say as a being of forces and energies. For instance, antibiotics and acupuncture must be regarded as not entirely physical activities; their effects upon the organism must be translated into energy actions in order to visualize the ramifications they are causing. This is the only way that we shall know whether they are adequate for dealing with the *whole* organism. Since it has been found essential to treat both primary and secondary causes in a patient, all therapists of whatever method *must* have a working knowledge of the spiritual, emotional, mental and physical realms, and be capable of advising on diet and other environmental factors. To do less is to store up possible trouble for the future. The other important factor that deserves mention is that any force applied, that is to say any treatment, must be gentle and unbiased so that the seeds of another disease process are not sown.

The other major issue of which all therapists should be aware is how to determine the point at which the disease has gone beyond possible reversal, that is to say become so complex or advanced that death is inevitable. This consideration highlights the other vital role of the healer: he must be able to ease a person's dying, making it as graceful as possible. By being aware of the time when further treatment is useless, he can then help the patient to reach acceptance and learn the lesson of dying. To try to contravene the natural laws and extend life at whatever cost, even with the best intentions in the world, is not in the true interest of the patient.

Promotion of Good Health

Because life and disease are not static, the promotion of good health is a progressive process. It is in this sphere that the individual is the only one who can take responsibility for his own health. Once again, awareness is of primary importance; awareness of self and of others. We are responsible for ourselves but we also have a collective responsibility. It is no use controlling our own systems perfectly if we, as a member of society, persist in poisoning our environment. It is equally pointless to perfect our environment if we then disregard our basic make-up and deny the needs of our own constitution.

Again the question of balance arises. Because we live in an imperfect world and are here to experience and develop, we should not over-emphasize any one sphere of our existence, but should try to maintain a continually-adjusted equilibrium within our lives. We are in a physical state and must abide by the laws that govern that state however much we may want to develop our psychological and spiritual selves. On the other hand we are not *only* physical beings, and we disregard the other parts of our being at our peril. To a large extent this balance is achieved by experience, so we must not expect to attain it easily or without making mistakes. Mistakes are made to be learned from, not to be bemoaned.

A major help in regulating our lives is to be positive in our thoughts, intentions and actions; indecision leads to negative influences. Having chosen a course of action that seems best to promote our well-being, we should follow it purposefully, monitoring our progress all the time. If things are not going according to plan, we must revise our original thoughts and form a new plan. We must be decisive although not rigid. Rigidity can promote disease by constraining us to pursue a course beyond its usefulness. This creates an unsympathetic environment, biases the organism and pressurizes it into a disease process.

Another factor essential to the promotion of good health is the development and use of our intuition. We must pay attention to those inner small voices which indicate that all is not well. They allow us to make fine adjustments within our self almost unconsciously, thus nipping in the bud potential disease. Coupled with this intuition must come the recognition of when we need help from others. Wise

43

selection of advice is of paramount importance and we should never be too proud or stubborn to seek and follow it.

Although doctors have always maintained that 'an ounce of prevention is better than a pound of cure', and that the need for treatment is in many cases an admission of failure, orthodox medicine has often failed in actively promoting good health because emphasis in the Western world has been on disregarding our bodies, except from an aesthetic and comfort point of view, until they go wrong. Doctors were primarily considered as repairers; and because they were very busy they accepted this role, although knowing that it was only part of their total function. Alternative practitioners have sometimes failed in this field for a different reason: some of their therapies are so new that they have not had time to explore beyond their immediate therapeutic methods. Now both schools of thought are recognizing, via different routes, the urgent need for prevention in a world which is becoming increasingly poisoned and unhealthy. Psychiatry, for instance, which only 25 years ago was a fringe medicine, has now become an intrinsic part of orthodoxy; by the curing of mental unbalance, much physical illness has been avoided. In the alternative field, patients are being taught prevention through diet, relaxation, meditation, etc.

Much time and money is now being spent by the medical world investigating various non-orthodox forms of treatment and developing new techniques from them. There is therefore general agreement that any method correctly applied has its place, that all avenues should be explored, and that many and differing techniques are necessary in order to procure the end result.

So important to our well-being is this topic that I feel it necessary to reiterate the individual's burden of responsibility. We are each responsible not only for our own good health, but also for that of others. We must become more aware of our own life systems and how they work. We must also be critically aware of how we fit into the network of life around us, and how we interact with other beings. Only thus have we any chance of promoting good health and minimizing disease. The failures that we experience along the way are not necessarily as negative as they first appear. They only become so when they are not recognized, or do not stimulate in us a desire to do better next time.

Differentiation of Therapies

We have reached the point now where we must explore the various therapies available in the Western World. An initial means of dividing them is as follows:

(A) Those that involve the taking of a remedy or the application of external materials.
(B) Those that require physical contact between the healer and the patient.
(C) Those that require the healer's presence.
(D) Those that can be carried out at a distance.
(E) Self-healing.

Of necessity there is some overlapping between the groups, especially as the exact nature of the therapies varies somewhat with the therapist.

GROUP A

1 Allopathy	Orthodox medicine.
2 Homoeopathy	System of prescribing based on the individuality of the patient, using minute doses of natural substances.
3 Bach Flower Remedies	Similar to homoeopathy but only remedies made from flowers are used and they are prepared differently.
4 Herbalism	Use of naturally grown and prepared plant extracts.
5 Hydrotherapy	Various uses of water.

6 Naturotherapy	Use of natural techniques and procedures (often a combination of various therapies).

GROUP B

1 Acupuncture	Use of special needles to interrupt and release energy flows.
2 Metamorphics (Pre-natal therapy)	Touching of points on the foot to release pre-natal and perinatal conditioning effects.
3 Kinesiology (Touch for Health)	Use of points on the body to release energy flows.
4 Osteopathy	Use of manipulative techniques to affect conditions of the body.
5 Cheiropraxis	Use of manipulative techniques to treat conditions of bones and joints.
6 Laying-on of Hands	Use of the hands to release and control energy flows in the body.
7 Acupressure	Use of acupuncture points using only finger pressure.
8 Physiotherapy	Use of contact stimulation of physical body.
9 Reflexology	Manipulation and pressure on the feet, to realign energy flows in specific organs.
10 Synergy Session	Use of acupressure combined with regression to release energy block.

11 Shiatsu	Combined acupressure and mobilization techniques to promote energy flow.
12 Rebirthing	Breathing technique causing patient to re-live birth experience in order to clarify and release negative life-patterns, followed by affirmations to produce positive patterns for the future.

GROUP C

1 Polarity (Magnetic) Healing	Using power of thought to balance energy systems.
2 Psychotherapy	Various techniques to release blocks of psychological origin.
3 Rational Emotive Therapy	Basically logical psychotherapy with stress on stimulation.
4 Transpersonal Psychology (Psychosynthesis)	Applying psychotherapy beyond the material existance.
5 Yoga	Various postural and breathing techniques.
6 Art Therapy	Art and painting used therapeutically.
7 Psychodrama	Use of drama to act out and release blocks in the psyche.
8 Gestalt Therapy	The acting out of problems.
9 Dance Therapy	Use of movement to release blockages.

10 Alexander Technique	Use of posture and movement to promote correct energy balance.
11 Counselling	Listening and advising.
12 Faith Healing	Use of religious faith to effect good energy flows.
13 Colour Therapy	Use of mental colour to stimulate normal energy flows.
14 Chromotherapy	Use of coloured lights.
15 Audiotherapy	Use of sound.
16 Hypnotherapy	Use of hypnosis to induce receptive state.
17 Dowsing (more commonly a diagnostic technique)	Use of the power of divining to correct energy flows.

GROUP D

1 Radionics	Use of dowsing power to project treatment via electronic emissions.
2 Distant Healing	Healing energy directed at an absent or geographically distant person through meditation or prayer.

GROUP E

1 Many of the above used by oneself.

2 Systems analysis and energy corrections.

3 Visualization techniques.

4 Meditation.

As well as these therapies, certain other non-orthodox techniques are available and used to aid diagnosis. These are as follows.

I Ching	Cheirology
Aura Reading	Iridology
Clairvoyance	Dreams
Clairaudience	Palmistry
Dowsing	Numerology
Biofeedback	The Runes
Phrenology	Radiaesthesia
Tarot	Physiognomy
Graphology	Biorhythms

We can see from this list that orthodox medicine is a very small part of the healing methods that man has available for treating disease. To me they *all* appear to have two things in common.

1 They all involve energy interchange and balancing.
2 *None* of them is perfect and covers all diseases, systems and individuals.

From these two common factors it would seem that any therapy given to a patient should not only correctly stimulate his energy flows and interactions, but should be especially chosen for him. For any given individual and his disease complex there will be several possible methods of treatment, but probably only one or two of these will be satisfactory. Selection of the best technique will therefore be a matter for extreme care, based not only on the requirements of the individual and his disease at that particular moment but also on his probable reaction to certain energies, depending on his personality, his background and his state of development.

Details of this selection process obviously cannot be tackled in a volume this size, but one thing about it becomes patently clear: to be a good therapist, whether your speciality is in alternative or orthodox medicine, you need a fair understanding of *all* the other techniques in order to chose the most suitable. Wherever possible, self-healing

49

should be our objective both as individuals and as a race.

The responsibility for the choice of therapy falls partly on the healer but also partly on the patient. No patient, and we are all potential ones, should accept *any* therapy before investigating its claims, its working, its limitations, its drawbacks and its dangers. He should also find out as much as possible about the individual therapist in question. The therapist should then satisfy himself, without consideration for his own pride, whether his specialty is really the most appropriate for the case. If it is not, this would imply no intrinsic deficiency in the therapy itself, but failure to recognize this could be dangerous.

Caution

There is a strong tendency in modern society to reduce all activities to logical technologies. This attitude is likely to have a very adverse effect when applied to human beings. One of the traps we should avoid therefore is changing the art of healing into a technology of healing. To some extent this undesirable situation already exists in orthodox medicine and there are signs of it happening to certain alternative, 'holistic' therapies. This must cease and the action be reversed if holistic medicine is to live up to its principles. This does not mean we should avoid the use of technology as an aid, but an aid it must remain.

Another necessary caution is not to lose sight of our goal in healing. The saving of life at all costs should definitely not be that goal. As death is a natural part of life, and the inevitable must happen sometime, part of the healer's responsibility is making the difficult decision as to when death should be allowed to take its course. Nor does his role stop there: he must also ensure that the passing from life be as smooth and gentle as possible. In the western world this role is almost always the prerogative of the orthodox practitioner, leaving the non-orthodox healer to take second place. The comfort of the patient's final days or hours therefore greatly depends on whether the doctor is a true healer or merely a medical technician. Death is a part of living and must be seen as such in order that it be given its correct perspective.

The question of over-treatment must also be considered. This applies to any form of therapy. It is only too easy to imagine that the more treatment given, the quicker will the patient recover. This is not so. For any given patient/illness there is an optimum amount of treatment. Up to this point there will be progressive improvement; beyond it there is likely to be none, or even an actual worsening of the condition. The intuition and awareness of the therapist provide the safety factor. An unaware, non-intuitive therapist is not in control of his powers and should be avoided. In conjunction with this caution we must also consider under-treatment. This again inevitably occurs where the therapist is either inexperienced, unaware, or not using his intuition. The results are not usually as dramatic as in over-treatment, but are very often the cause of a simple disease becoming chronic or progressive. Insufficient stimulation, or stimulation at the wrong time or place, merely disguise the patient's true state. The patient must also play his part by becoming more self-aware so that he can intelligently and sensitively report back to his healer. He can also help enormously by adopting a receptive attitude, feeling hopeful, and following any advice he may be given about diet, exercise, etc.

Another caution is against the use of conflicting remedies. Some remedies are compatible, others are antagonistic, while yet others are synergistic, that is to say they require each other in order to produce their optimal effect. In the first instance the compatible remedies mix well and can both help, although it is not essential to use them together. In the second case, antagonistic remedies either work against each other or compete for the same site of action, thus effectively producing undertreatment. The third type on the contrary should always be given simultaneously. The issue is complicated, however, by the fact that in some patient/disease complexes, remedies may fall into one of these groups, whereas in another of the same nature, these same remedies fall into another group.

51

Here is another case where intuition and awareness as well as knowledge are required.

Another obvious major danger is that of misdiagnosis. Many disease conditions appear outwardly to be the same, yet have different origins and modes of action. Where faulty diagnosis occurs, it is because the therapist tries to pigeon-hole conditions arbitrarily without using his own faculties of perception. There is really no excuse for this happening except where the healer is very inexperienced or the disease exceptionally multifaceted.

This short survey covers most of the things that can go wrong in treatment. It is less likely to be the healer with an orthodox training who produces these problems, because long years of study and the attendant experience tend to safeguard him. The non-orthodox therapist does however at times succumb to these pitfalls unless humility and caution are his. There is one glaring exception: that of iatrogenic disease. Here, almost without exception, orthodox medicine is to blame. If the full possible effects of a new drug are not known, all sorts of disaster may follow its use. The remedy may well initially have its desired effect on the patient, but at the same time it may be having gross distorting effects on all his or her other bodies, causing imbalance to the whole organism. These new imbalances declare themselves as 'side effects'. Whenever side effects occur, beware. They contain within themselves manifold possibilities of future diseases. Sometimes this is a calculated risk worth taking, *but not often.*

I think that it is important here briefly to mention a particular aspect of death. In order that there should exist a dynamic state, capable of evolution rather than a static state producing no progress, death is necessary, and can be envisaged as a release of borrowed energy which will then return to source. Whether or not we believe in any sort of 'after-life', this applies.

The following four cardinal points should help us avoid most of the problems and dangers inherent in treatment:

1 Evidence of disease in any function of a patient is an

52

indication that the organism as a whole is inharmoniously balanced. Look to restore a normal balance, no more.

2 Attacking disease through one system alone and disregarding the others may produce multiple complications, (e.g. dealing with physical disease in isolation may change one of the patient's other factors so drastically that a 'new' disease manifests).

3 Treating only one aspect of an individual at a time may result in a temporary benefit only or no benefit at all, (e.g. treating anaemia without ensuring an adequate dietic supply of iron will ultimately result in failure, although a temporary relief may occur though the mobilization of body iron stores).

4 Treating disease with remedies that have possible unknown effects, or side-effects, may lead to disaster, (e.g. treating only the physical aspects of hypertension may result in the breakdown of the patient's mental, emotional and/or spiritual health).

Responsibility

The big question in healing is one of responsibility. Who is to promote health? What is the healer's role? What is the patient's role?

Modern doctors originated in the healing fraternities of the past, when common healers banded together to break the rigid and biased stranglehold of the priest/healers. In doing so they eventually created for themselves a new and equally rigid trap. The old, empirical ways were swept aside, although not without a struggle, and scientific knowledge became the criterion of good practice. There has recently been a move away from this total rigidity, but many doctors still only allow their patients access to those methods which have a scientifically provable basis. They are technological-doctors rather than artist-doctors. By not permitting their intuition to develop, or else denying its existence altogether, they are refusing the full responsibility of their positions. Unless orthodox medicine can change in this respect soon, it is doomed to play a very minor role in future therapeutics.

One of the biggest obstacles to such a change at present is financial. Too much money has been committed to the technology of medicine for it to capitulate without a battle to cheaper, subtler methods. I feel sure however that enough true healer/doctors remain to combat and eventually overcome Big Business.

To return to our original question: what are the roles of the healer and of the patient? Once the healer has divined the existence of the disease and has provided the initial impetus to the healing energies, he then acts merely as comptroller to ensure that the desired effect, and *only* the desired effect is produced. It is then up to the patient. Ultimately it is only he who can cure himself. His relationship with the healer, which should be two-way and growing all the time, will support him, but the healer can do nothing unless the patient is willing to take responsibility for his own growth and well-being.

3 Healing in the Judeo-Christian Tradition

Turning now from the medical outlook on healing, we come to a description and history of healing as found in the Bible and as interpreted by a clergyman of the Church of England who is himself a practising healer.

The Concept of Wholeness

The book of Genesis and the creation story start with the concept of Wholeness. Outwardly the story describes the six days of Creation as the six phases in which life appeared and evolved on this planet; inwardly it is telling us the most fundamental truths about life, its meaning and purpose, and man's place within the complex whole. Whether life arrived on earth with a big bang or evolved over millions of years is not important for this discussion. What is vital is the concept very clearly stated in Genesis that the original basis of Creation was harmony and the peaceful interdependance of all God's creatures.

Man, created in the image of God and therefore intrinsically good, was aware of the Whole and of his place within it. He was given, by direct command, responsibility for maintaining the ecological balance between all the diversities within the Unity. The Garden of Eden

55

represents then this concept of the unifying, harmonious inter-relationship between all life forms. There man's food and that of the animal kingdom must of necessity be vegetarian, because harmony cannot exist where one member of a whole is living at the expense of another.

This idea, incidentally, is one of the paths by which many enlightened people, especially the rising generation, are returning to this fundamental idea of Wholeness. Through true meditation and contemplation they are finding that to kill and eat animals is both unnecessary and repulsive. In a growing sense of relationship with all life forms, with the All in all, they are seeing the suffering of animals in intensive livestock farming as not only distasteful but also as undesirable for the health of the planet. Seen from the point of view of a more equable feeding of mankind, they also condemn the growing of meat protein as being a wasteful form of food production.

The next phase in the story of man's development is that of Adam and Eve becoming aware of the natural energies and of their ability to use or misuse their control over these. Through the eating of the fruit from the 'tree of the knowledge of good and evil', a new state of consciousness is born in man. He gains the ability to be retrospective and anticipatory. He can now choose between being either the selfless agent of harmony and interdependence, or being the exploiting, self-centred acquisitor, consequently separated from the Whole of which he is intrinsically part.

By having chosen the latter role and contributed to fragmentation and dis-ease, man finds himself also firmly placed in the central position of active healing agent consciously obliged to recover and sustain balance and harmony for survival. 'For God doth know that in the day that ye eat thereof, then your eyes shall be opened, and ye shall be as gods, knowing good and evil.' These polarities, of which man becomes gradually more aware, are represented in the Bible as God and Satan the Tester. By accepting the burden of choice and self-determination, man is lifted up above the more primitive forms of life and

56

consciousness which unquestioningly perform the functions for which they are created because they know no alternative.

This suggests that man creates his own un-ease, which then manifests at the physical level as disease. This does not however make the individual entirely responsible for his or her dis-ease because 'The sins of the fathers are visited upon the children unto the third and fourth generation, but mercy is shown to thousands (of generations) to them that love God and keep His commandments.' (Exodus 20: 5 and 6.) We inherit though our genes, our conditioning and our parenting, but the pattern of cause and effect can be broken due to this God-given gift of choice. We *can* heal ourselves. We are capable of restoring balance to ourselves and ultimately to the entire world.

The concept of wholeness is not only an intellectual concept; it is the reality within which, in moments of enlightenment, man has seen his part within creation. I am referring to 'the mystic experience of the oneness of all creation', which is the foundation experience behind all the great world religions. Through the ages men and women have either worked towards it through meditation and contemplation, or have stumbled upon it in moments of great tranquility. It is not uncommon, nor is it confined to the great saints and mystics. It has been described as the silence that is true 'Communion', when all breaches are healed, there is no sense of separation, and there is awareness of timeless, indestructible 'security'. It is to be at one with The One that is All in all.

Health Through the Law

Judaism has been described as a religion of the Law based upon this concept of creation. In the first five books of the Bible, or Torah, are embodied the rules governing the religious practices and the social and moral life of the Israelites, including rules of hygiene, diet and quarantine. The Torah which is read in Synagogue every Sabbath is divided into two distinct categories: the concept of creation, which is regarded as coming from Supreme Authority or God; and the laws, rituals and disciplines to maintain that which is of God.

So the Law is about the pattern of Creation into which human life and behaviour must fit if harmony is to be achieved and the well-being of the individual and society maintained. The Law maintaining 'The Divine Harmony', being God-given, is unalterable; the Law governing human behaviour changes as human consciousness evolves and social life becomes more gentle and civilized.

When Jesus quotes the 'summary of the Law', or our first two Commandments, He maintains that it is the key to a quality of life that the Bible calls Eternal. If you listen, or attend, with every fibre of your being, you will become aware of the One of which you are a part, and a relationship will be established between you and that which is beyond words. And the clue, the essence of that relationship is love, out of which will come healing and the restoration of wholeness.

To obey God then brings well-being; to disobey brings discord and disease. Sin and sickness appear to be inseparable. The origin of the word 'sin' in the Hebrew means 'missing the mark'. It implies being out of tune with the Divine Harmony. Repentance implies re-thinking and correcting one's aim, and tuning in to the Creative Intelligence within the Cosmos.

In the early stage of the Jewish people's history, healing was entirely concerned with God, and with people's relationship to Him and to the Divine order. It was only the priests and the prophets, as chosen mediators of the Divine Will, who were entitled to act in this area.

It was to the priest that a man went for confirmation of his disease; it was the priest who later provided proof of cure and declared him free from infection and quarantine. All purification rites connected with childbirth, menstruation and the recovery from venereal disease were conducted by the temple authorities. The greatest Prophets such as Elijah and Elisha are reported to have reached such excellence in healing that they no longer needed to use their hands or herbs or other external agents, but were able to heal through inner spiritual transformation. In certain cases such as that of Hezekiah, a total repentance, some inner metamorphosis, allowed him to be given a further fifteen years of life in order to fulfill a special function allotted to him by God.

The Old Testament attitude towards healing and the few physicians who were not priests is well summed up in the story of King Asa who in the thirty ninth year of his reign was stricken with a disease in his feet (gangrene?). It is said that 'He sought not to the Lord but to physicians' and died a couple of years later. The suggestion is that in going to a physician instead of a priest he displayed a lack of faith and was punished.

It is interesting to note that there is no Hebrew equivalent to our idea of the physical body. Man was considered as a whole, and the various aspects of that whole were never thought of in isolation. Man was an undivided entity of body, mind and Spirit, with health an equally undivided entity of balance, harmony and fulfilment. Obedience to God's law was rewarded by the outward and visible signs of strength and long life, strength here meaning a strong, dignified character. This concept of an undivided entity, strongly dependent for health on its own moral fibre, is one that has, sadly, been mainly lost in modern medicine. Under pressure of circumstances, doctors and therapists today tend to become body mechanics, that is almost entirely preoccupied with the mechanisms and chemistry of the physical body.

The Hebrew word Shalom is perhaps the one which expresses most closely this concept of health. Although translated in English as 'peace' it means far more than a state of not being at war; it encompasses in fact the entire ideal of human endeavour: completeness, soundness, prosperity untouched by violence or misfortune, individual and community harmony, and consequent physical health.

The Role of Priests and Physicians in Healing

The geographical position of the tiny land of Israel made it a bottleneck through which passed the great caravan routes from the East. The wisdom, culture and understanding of Egypt, Babylonia, Assyria, Persia, Greece and Rome were instrumental in forming the brilliant and advanced state of understanding of the Jewish people. To this absorbing and transforming process the intelligentsia and the mystics gave a spiritual foundation, writing and teaching and interpreting religion, and therefore healing, at countless different levels. Because the knowledge remains largely in the guardianship of holy men, the priests and prophets, it is referred to as 'esoteric' or hidden, and this it must largely remain because much of it such as the cyphers, codes and sound vibrations which carry creative healing potential, can also be misused to disintegrate and destroy. The knowledge remained esoteric in part because it was powerful and capable of misuse, but mainly because it was received by 'divine revelation'. To share it at the intellectual level could well deprive the experience of the Divine Presence that should accompany it. The things of God reveal themselves when man is mature enough to receive them. Initiation into 'The Mysteries' is therefore part of one's natural maturing through rightly-handled experiences of life.

If we move on to the second century B.C. and refer to the writings in the Apochrypha, we discover a less rigid attitude towards healing and a more trusting relationship between the authorities and the general public. The word Apocrypha is derived from a Greek word and really means 'the hidden things'. These writings usually appear as a separate section between the Old and New Testaments; if not, they are readily available as a separate publication.

Because of its great beauty, and because it clarifies the attitudes prevailing before the birth and ministry of Jesus, a reference to Ecclesiasticus is helpful. Chapter 38 emphatically demands that we honour the physician and accept his services, for his skills are from God. Reference is then made to the healing potential of herbs and natural substances as another God-given gift. So are the skills available through the apothecary. The principle remains clear that disease is a signal of inner discord, and that if inner harmony at psychological, emotional and spiritual level is recovered, that is to say Shalom, then we will receive help at the chemico-physical level to expedite the rebalancing of the body, which will then reflect that harmony and do what it is created to do.

During the second and first centuries B.C. there existed monastic communities now referred to as the Qumran type communities, because of the one at Qumran where the famous Dead Sea scrolls were recently uncovered. These communities followed a rule of poverty and obedience. Springing out of a Jewish movement known as the Hasidim or Holy Ones, they were a disciplined, prayerful group within orthodox Judaism. Later the Essenes followed their example and were strong at the time of John the Baptist and Jesus.

These communities, in which purity, selflessness and high ethical standards prevailed, took over the guardianship of the knowledge hidden beneath the words of Torah. They studied the effects of mind upon matter and the interactions between Spirit, mind, soul, psyche and the physical body. They examined such phenomena as astrology, psychic powers and healing energies. They sought to understand what lay behind the concept of angels and spiritualism and the influences exercised by these entities and forces. Everything that we today call the 'occult' and the 'esoteric' was part of their research. What they uncovered was a catalogue of information and techniques capable of being used for either good or evil, for healing or for destruction. These inheritors of the Mysteries, and of the hidden wisdom of Kabbalah, tended to become an exclusive élite; they were in no sense evangelistic.

In contrast to the intellectual seekers typified by the Essenes, there have always existed those loving people who radiate healing and that 'peace which passes all understanding' through natural goodness and a highly developed intuitive sense. Without any knowledge of the mechanics of healing, they just know that it is available, and that harmony is the intended condition for us all. It may well be that these 'innocents' are the most trustworthy and effective of all healers.

Jesus as Healer

Within the Christian church there exist those who attain this ability to heal through their relationship with the man Jesus. In examining the approach taken by Him, the question arises as to which school of healing He fits into. Reading Chapter 11 of St. Matthew, one inclines to the view that Jesus favoured the natural intuitive approach: 'I thank Thee O Father, Lord of Heaven and earth because Thou hast hid these things from the wise and prudent, and hast revealed them unto babes'. He clearly regarded natural goodness and the innocence of 'babes' as a prerequisite to being a good healer. Furthermore He seems to warn us that scientific, esoteric and occult practises are safe only in the hands of men with high moral standards.

Before moving on to the work of Jesus the healer, it would be rewarding to look at the Nativity story considered from the point of view of two possible approaches to wisdom and thence to healing, because the ways in which the shepherds and the Wise Men found Jesus are analogous to the two different ways in which healers can find their path. The shepherds, natural intuitive men who possessed that animal radar system which we call the psychic faculty, were the first to arrive at the stable. Their sensitivity and essential innocence had responded to the event. Their journey was short and direct. The Wise Men, Magi, or magicians on the other hand had long and roundabout journeys. Through astrology, the ancient wisdom and various scientific techniques, coupled with consciously-developed psychic powers, they too arrived at the same goal as the Shepherds, but they arrived later.

Although Jesus no doubt knew about the Magi approaches to healing, it was by the shepherds' way that He reached the completeness of His human potential. It would seem that Jesus' approach to healing was that of fundamental – though divinely inspired – love and understanding; the way for the common man. When He refers to Himself as 'The Son of Man', He is identifying Himself with that which is born out of our humanity. What He achieved as a human being and healer, we can ultimately achieve.

In order to understand Jesus and penetrate the depth of His healing, one must understand his background and His roots and see Him as the product of the most traditional Judaism. Although certain modern writers assert that Jesus studied with the Essenes, Jewish historians and Rabbis, together with most Christian theologians, agree that there is no evidence of Jesus using the healing techniques taught and practised by the Essenes. Jewish opinion places Him as the true heir of an age-old prophetic religious line. His teaching and practices, they say, reflect the influence of the Hasidim or devout, who believed prayer to be all-powerful, capable of performing miracles.

This view of Jesus is foretold in Chapter 11 of Isaiah where the coming of the Christ is seen as restoring harmony to the individual and re-establishing wholeness in creation. In Verse 6: 'The wolf shall dwell with the lamb and the leopard shall lie down with the kid', we understand that no friction or splintering can exist where wholeness is to be.

Salvation, the word frequently used as the translation of the Greek 'soteria' (which literally means 'safe and sound' or 'healthy') would come, so the Jews anticipated, via an anointed prince. A word or two on this is appropriate as the powerful symbolism of anointing with oil is now used by the Christian church in its healing ritual, and was then used for appointing the Kings of Israel, who were regarded as Priest Kings, mediators of the Divine Will. In the sacrament of anointing – and a sacrament is an outward and visible sign of an inward and spiritual grace – oil is of great significance, for it is distilled by fire. So it is through the

63

refining and strengthening fires of adversity that spiritual strength is bestowed. Until Jesus had been subjected to adversity, He could not be baptised by the fire of the Holy Spirit, that is He could not be whole and bring Salvation to others.

All of this may help to explain the way in which Jesus introduces Himself and His healing ministry after going through the 'Temptations in the Wilderness' and His Baptism in the Jordan. On His return to Nazareth, the place of His upbringing, He is accorded the privilege of reading the Scripture and giving a short discourse on it.

From Chapter 61, verses 1 and 2 He reads the description of the anticipated Messiah: 'The Spirit of the Lord is upon Me, because He hath anointed Me to preach the gospel to the poor, He hath sent Me to heal the broken hearted, to preach deliverance to the captives, and the recovering of sight to the blind, to set at liberty them that are bruised and to preach the acceptable year of the Lord.'

With the eyes of everyone upon Him, Jesus closes the book and says to the congregation, 'This day is this Scripture fulfilled in your ears.'

Taking one item at a time, we shall see how fully Jesus accomplished this mission.

First of all He offered salvation to ordinary men and women instead of following the custom of the ancient cultures where knowledge of 'spiritual realities' was confined to the Initiates. Highly developed human beings were not expected to appear from the ranks of the common man, yet Jesus did not chose His Apostles from the élite, and He spent much time in so-called bad company, transforming the lives of 'publicans and sinners'.

In 'healing the broken-hearted', Jesus gave men the strength and the spiritual resources to overcome life's circumstances instead of being subject to them.

By preaching 'deliverance to the captive' He released those who were imprisoned in their psychological patterns, very much as Jung later sought to free us from all that imprisons us and prevents us from being our true selves. This deliverance can also include exorcisms to free a person

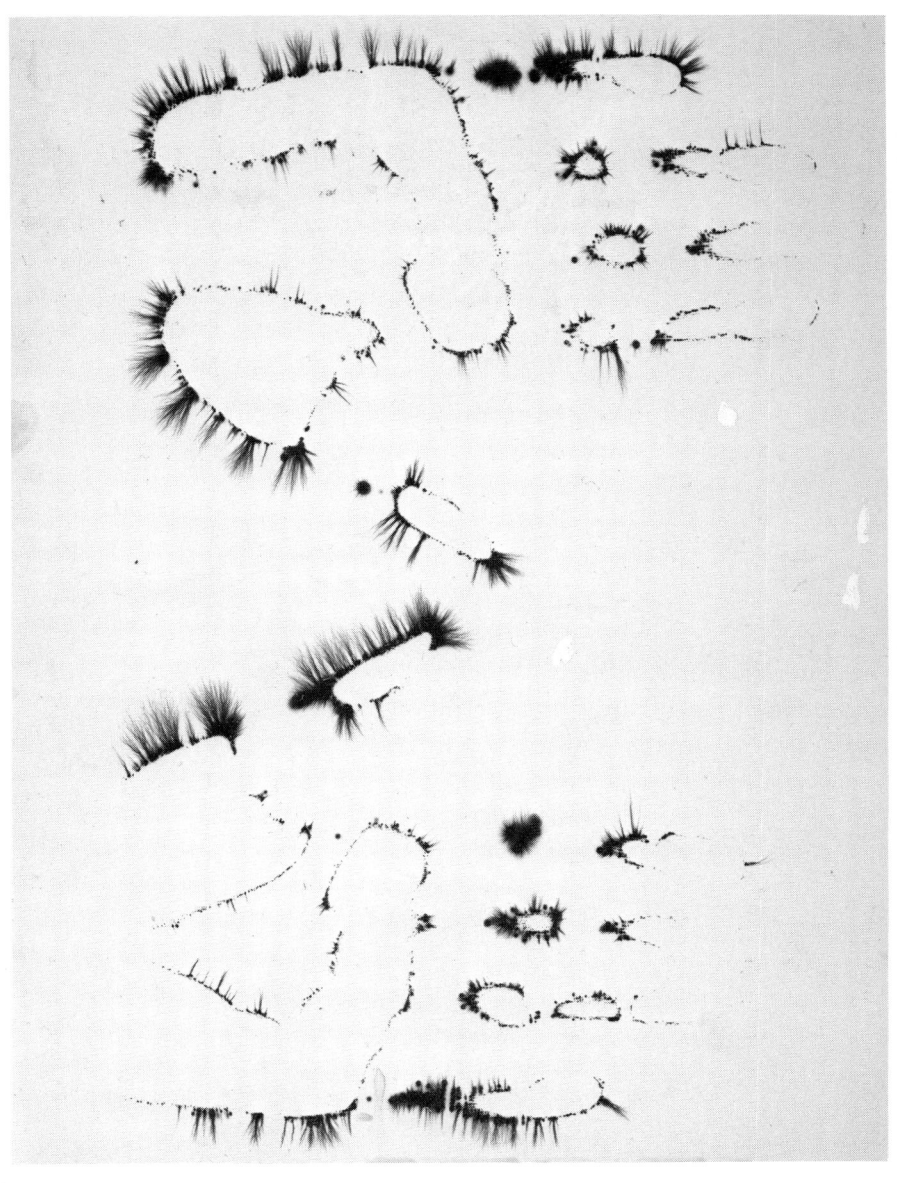

Plate 1 – Kirlian photograph   The hands of a withdrawn person. Note the lack of energy-radiations from the fingers.

Plate 2 – Kirlian photograph The hands of a client before healing. The life-energy is very low.

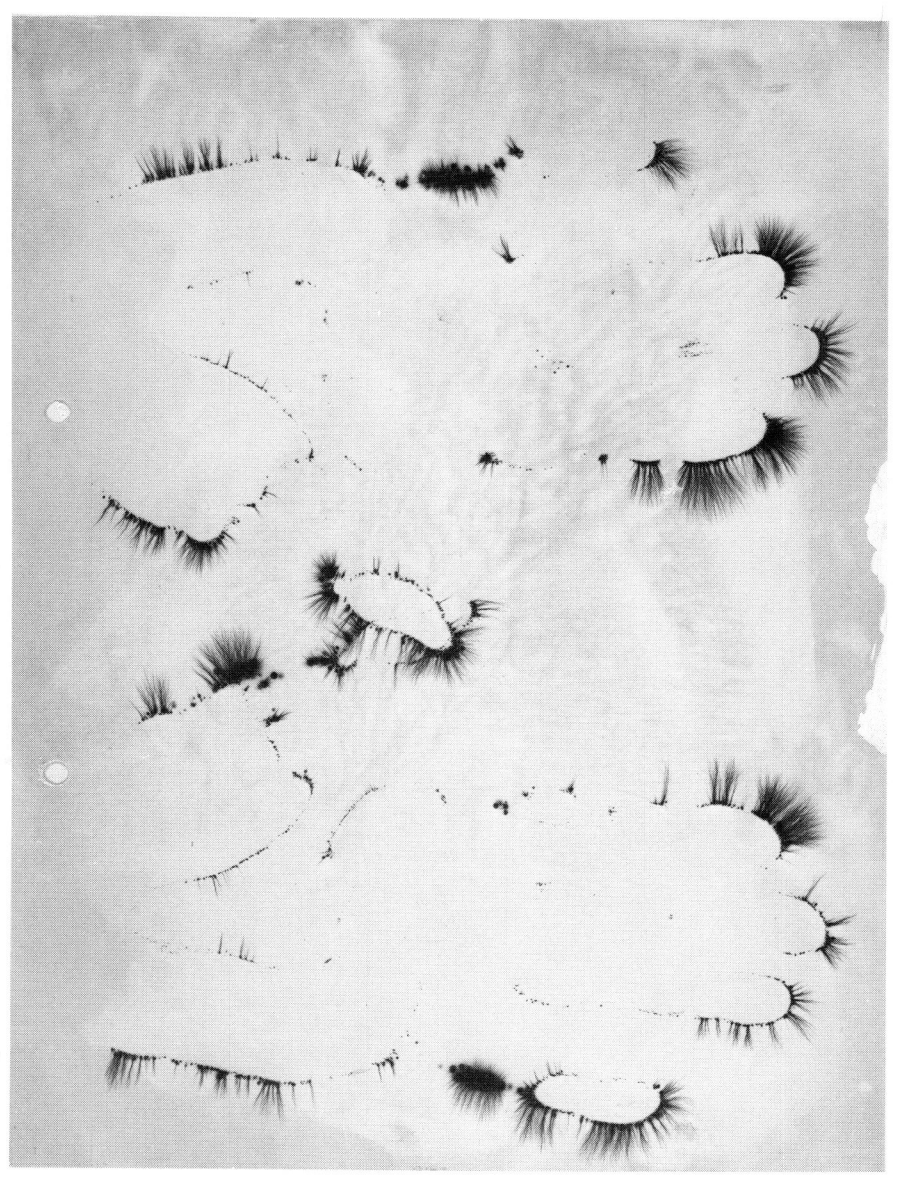

Plate 3 – Kirlian photograph The hands of the same client after half an hour of healing. There is noticeably more energy in the aura, particularly around the fingertips, and the palms are becoming visible.

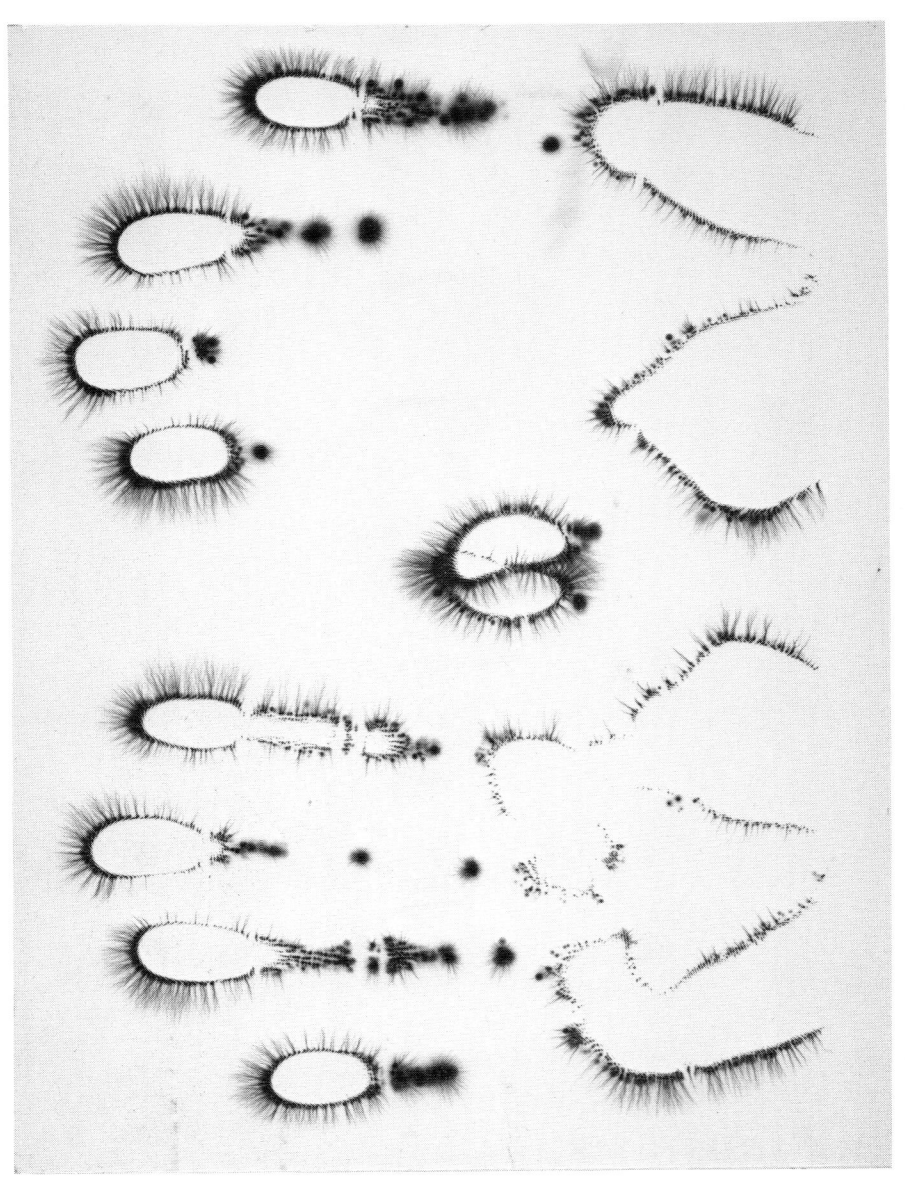

Plate 4–Kirlian photograph The hands of a balanced person. Note the regularity of the inner corona (dark band surrounding fingertips) and of the 'splines' or rays.

from possession by devils or by discarnate entities. With a commanding presence and voice of absolute authority Jesus dealt frequently with such conditions.

He healed physical blindness, but He also opened peoples' eyes to truth, and enabled them to develop the Spirit of Discernment. By 'setting at liberty the bruised,' He healed people who were consciously or unconsciously nursing emotional and psychological injuries and buried memories which prevented their growth into maturity.

The term 'the acceptable year of the Lord' seems to mean the age of enlightenment initiated for mankind by the life and teaching of Jesus. Within three centuries Christianity would influence the whole of the civilized world.

To suggest that one man could simultaneously be a physical healer, a psychotherapist, an exorcist and a transformer of mens' material, social and political motives, would appear to be an excessive claim. Yet the healing ministry of Jesus can effect the individual at every level and reach beyond the personal stage to a social and national one. In the acceptable year of the Lord the nations were ripe for healing and for reforming the family of man under the Fatherhood of God.

Spiritual Healing

This universality of healing is the claim made by true Spiritual healing when done in 'the name of Jesus Christ'. To understand the significance of 'names' in Jewish thought and the Hebrew language, one must realize that in every Hebrew proper name is a description of the person or place. For example, Jerusalem means Foundation or Abode of Peace; Jesus is another name for Joshua or Salvation; and Messias or Messiah, Christ, means anointed. This term was originally used for anyone who was anointed with holy oil, but later it referred exclusively to The Anointed One who would come to rescue and redeem Israel, as foretold by the prophets. So to heal 'In the name of Jesus Christ' means in the name of all the characteristics and attributes represented by Jesus, who was able to say, 'I and the Father are One'.

Because He can say this, Jesus can further say 'Where two or three are gathered together in My Name, there I am in the midst of them'. Jehova or Jaweh means *I am*. Jehovah also means God. So by invoking the name or help of Jesus we can call into our midst the presence of God to commune with and manifest in man. If two or three people come together to express the characteristics of love, harmony and beauty and all that is present in Jesus Christ, another dimension also present is Jaweh, the *I am*. From this presence will come re-creation and re-forming; the whole healing of a person will take place.

The writer has frequently encountered natural healers, working in the name of Jesus Christ, who have been amazed by the complete harmonizing of character and family relationships accompanying their patients' physical healing.

There is a good example of this in the miracle of the man sick of the palsy. When Jesus says to him, 'Son, be of good cheer; thy sins be forgiven thee,' the scribes (the interpreters of the Law) felt that this was blasphemy. But Jesus simply commanded the paralysed man to walk, thereby telling us that He equated forgiveness of sins with release or healing, and that He saw little difference between the inner healing and its physical manifestation. Once the man's sin was no longer making him 'miss the mark', he would inevitably be able to free himself from physical paralysis.

Jesus used both words and touch in order to heal. He also gave distant healing as in the case of the Roman Centurion who so believed in His healing power that he knew one word or thought from Jesus would suffice to cure his child. It is said that Jesus marvelled at such faith, particularly in one who was not Jewish. Here He saw that 'the Name' would transcend the boundaries of culture, race, and even religion.

Schism between Christianity and Judaism

The split between the followers of Jesus and Judaism occurs over the question of the expectations placed on the Messiah. The Jews cannot accept that Jesus fulfilled these expectations. Many Jews hold Jesus in the greatest respect, but they see Him *only* as an heir to the prophetic line of Hasidim. As one Rabbi put it to me with a kindly smile, 'It was a near miss, a very near miss, but a miss!'

This question is not answerable by intellectual argument and theological debate. It is only answered by one's own experience, and by whether His truth is manifested in the lives of people who claim to have come under His continuing influence. To quote the German philosopher, Nietzche, 'These Christians must show me they are redeemed before I will believe in their redeemer'.

For His part, Jesus constantly drew attention away from Himself and His personality to the *I am*, to the Father within, whose work He was doing and through whom man could recapture his spiritual origins and fulfil his purpose as healing agent within creation. The term New Testament or New Covenant refers to this new and binding relationship between man and God achieved by Jesus and available to all through Him.

Those who could absorb all that He represented would, He said, be like salt. The salt in food is the unseen element which draws out the true flavour of the whole, and is noticeable mainly by its absence. In order for us to be truly human it is essential, of the essence, that we contain the unseen element of the Christ. At another time He compared the Christ within to the leaven in the dough. This invisible element in society would lift the level of human dignity in a way which could never be achieved otherwise.

Gradually Jesus' role as the mediator, the link between man and God, became the essential of this New Covenant, creating unbearable tensions within Judaism. As Jesus had forecast, the new wine was to burst the old bottles.

Holy Communion: The Healing Service

With Jesus as the key to the Divine Harmony, the Apostles, and later the converts, inherited His gifts of healing. Where response or faith made it possible, they channelled this Harmony to the disorientated and the diseased. This emphasis on healing was incorporated within the central ritual of Holy Communion which gave the new Christian movement purity and a common purpose.

The Eucharist, Holy Communion or Mass has its origins in the Last Supper which Jesus shared with His disciples. It is a ritual grown out of the Jewish Chaverah, or Chakurah, or meeting of friends, a ritual meal held in Jewish homes on the eve of the Sabbath or any great Jewish Festival. It still continues today with the same prayers and thanksgivings as those spoken by Jesus.

At the Last Supper, however, Jesus added words of His own which must have been both challenging and dramatic. When the guests were all seated, He took a loaf in His hands and offered the familiar Blessing and Thanksgiving, 'Blessed art Thou O Lord our God Eternal King, Who bringeth forth bread from the earth.' But then, instead of continuing with the well-known ritual, Jesus added words of His own, 'Take and eat this, this is My body which is given for you.' In other words, everything that has been given to you through My physical being is to be absorbed into your being. I shall be arrested, tried, crucified, and dis-membered only to be re-membered in you. And through My healing will come the healing of the world.

'Do this in remembrance of Me', He continued. 'Become the continuing instrument of My purposes; become the Body of Christ, the true Church.'

Then after supper He took the cup, the loving cup, and spoke the familiar thanksgiving, 'Blessed art Thou O Lord our God, Eternal King, Who fillest the whole earth with Thy goodness.'

Again Jesus added His own words, 'Drink of it, for this is My blood of the New Covenant which is shed for many for the remission of sins.' Again He promises healing through forgiveness, drawing on the age-old significance of Blood as Life, the Enabling Force.

So the Last Supper, the central drama of the Christian Church, is seen as a healing service which Jesus instituted for the restoration of the wholeness which He represents and makes available to all those who can respond and receive. The only vital prerequisite is repentance, or the acknowledgement of one's own dis-ease and disorientation. This applies also to one's preparation for such rituals as the Laying on of Hands and Holy Unction. The use of powerful, archetypal symbols in ritualized healing services must not be allowed to detract from the simple unencumbered healing phenomena that frequently occur where two or three gather in His Name. Both forms of healing have their place, but simplicity is the keynote of Jesus' healing.

There are members of the orthodox church who maintain that healing should only be practised by the ordained ministry. This point of view does not stem only from the Churches' fear for their authority; there are traps and delusions for those who discover and practise their healing gifts. One of these traps lies in a natural but often mistaken desire to see physical healing take place. If a healer or a healing group concentrate their power on achieving physical restoration only, then everything which the diseased body has been signalling about the patient's inner life and relationships will be disregarded, and inevitably a new manifestation of the original imbalance will have to occur, usually within a few months.

There are also, however, traps within the most formalized and orthodox healing services, where a group mind can quite unconsciously become so emotionally charged and so dominated by the will of the leader empowered by the group, that the Christian prayer 'Thy will be done, not mine,' becomes lost. Once again, healing can occur in such circumstances, but it will not be balanced and lasting as it will have been born out of emotionalism and man's will as opposed to the will of God.

Psychic Healing

We should next take a brief look at psychic faculties and psychic healing. An increasing number of people are discovering that they have these latent faculties, which in the writer's experience are frequently present in those who have had an isolated, lonely, or very painful childhood,

69

and who were consequently dependant on their 'animal radar system' for survival. I use this term because most of us know examples of psychic behaviour in animals: a cat which always knows when its owner is returning from holiday, or a horse which stopped dead or shied at the site of former violence. There are frequent stories about dogs giving a pitiful howl at the exact moment of their masters' death.

The extrasensory powers of perception seem to be a natural part of our human faculties; they can be either useful or completely disorientating. This appears to depend on whether the individual becomes subject to these experiences or whether he is in control of them and capable of using them constructively and lovingly. I refer to such faculties as the power of mind over matter as demonstrated by Uri Geller (psychokinesis); contact with the memory bank of places and objects (psychometry); thought reading and transference etc. (telepathy); the ability to see energy fields in the form of refracted light or auras, which is very useful for detection of disease at all levels; the power to see or hear people no longer possessing a physical body (clairvoyance and clairaudience).

There are branches of the Church which state categorically that these faculties should be ignored and not brought into use in Christian healing. There are also true Christians who experience and use these faculties creatively in the name of Jesus Christ. Amongst the latter are many who have devoted their lives to prayer, meditation and contemplation within various monasteries and convents.

It may not be necessary when dealing with hauntings, poltergeists, possession and psychic disorders, to understand and experience all the above phenomena, but many who find themselves engaged in this area of healing are there because they are psychically aware.

Some Christian healers, whether or not they understand the mechanics of what is happening, display in themselves both the shepherd and the Magi stream of healing, the intuitive and the psychic. In this age of scientific enlightenment, this will become increasingly common. The extended awareness and highly developed insights of Jesus show us the result of every human faculty being completely developed; we have in Him the example to which we must aspire in order to achieve the ultimate in healing.

This completeness has been achieved by certain outstanding individuals whose lives and healing work were such that Ecclesiastical authority has pronounced their work miraculous, and the individuals have become Saints.

Often this saintliness manifests in humble unassuming people such as Bernadette the simple peasant girl whose 'vision' of the Blessed Virgin utterly transformed and purified her. The Wholeness created in the place where the vision occurred made Lourdes a 'door', a focal point through which people are led to the Christ. Once again, as in individual healing, its efficacy depends to some extent upon the attitudes and expectations of the pilgrims.

Medicine and the Concept of Wholeness

This need for wholeness, always recognized by the Church, is increasingly taken into account by modern medicine. A doctor once told me that after forty years as a general practitioner, he was convinced that over ninety per cent of his patients suffered from diseases that were psychosomatic in origin. He believed that if a person lives in a constant state of tension through business pressures, unsatisfactory personal relationships and so on, this un-ease inevitably manifests as dis-ease at the physical level.

Medicine today, so influenced by scientific materialism, has tended to consider only the physical body, or at best the physical and psychological bodies. Heavily pressurized by the demands of the National Health Service, doctors have no time for relating to the patient as a whole. But there is a growing revolt amongst young doctors and scientists at being cast in the role of body mechanics. Many of them who were unconsciously called to a healing profession as a result of their developing sensitivity and awareness are responding eagerly to the new spiritual enlightenment.

71

This implies that the patient will now be allowed, or rather encouraged, to take co-responsibility with the doctor for his or her condition. It also implies the need for increasing awareness of ourselves. Part of the healing process will of necessity entail coming to terms with our anxieties, insecurities, fears, buried memories of deep emotional hurt, and accumulated reservoirs of anger and resentment.

The Mystic Experience

There has been much research of late into the proposition of 'Everlasting Life', of continuing consciousness after the death of the physical body. The collected experiences of people who have been revived from death by up-to-date scientific techniques are reassuring. The transition from one world to another begins to lose its terror, and become a thing of wonder and beauty.

Psychic research into communication with those who have 'died' also demands increasing attention, causing many to accept the Reincarnationist's view of life as a long-term learning process.

Many have also enjoyed deep inner experiences confirming the truths under consideration so that they become an inner *knowing* instead of intellectually acceptable propositions. All this helps to reassure us and ease the basic sense of insecurity which so undermines wholeness.

To work through to the complete security which is the foundation of wholeness, there is a further step to be taken. That is to grasp the meaning of eternal life, and so discover the spiritual core of our being, that divine spark which is timeless.

Albert Schweitzer, the great doctor and contemporary mystic, describes this reality as follows: 'Mysticism is present whenever a man looks upon the separation between earth and Heaven, time and eternity as overcome, and feels while yet in earth and time, as though he had entered into Heaven and Eternity.'

In Jesus' terms this step means that 'The Kingdom of God is at hand', or 'As the lightning flash, so comes the Son of Man'. This implies that divine harmony is a reality which is ever-present and can be instantaneously revealed to us.

In the words of one contemporary spiritual healer, 'The miraculous occurs when that which is present all the time breaks through to human consciousness.'

What Jesus says is that we are no longer subject to the laws of cause and effect; we need no longer be imprisoned within our karma. By stepping out of our linear thinking and the 'illusions' of time and space we can find the 'still point of the turning world, the point of intersection between the times and time,' as described by St. Thomas Aquinas. This is the goal of all true meditation. From this 'inner core' of our being we are able to deal with the circumstances of life rather than be subject to them.

The end result of this awakening, says Jesus, is joy. 'Ask and ye shall receive, that your Joy may be full.' (John 16:24,6.) Happiness depends upon external happenings; joy transcends happenings. Those who have experienced this for even a few fleeting moments would maintain that here lies the key to wholeness, and that no healing is secure unless it takes into account the reality which lies behind the term 'eternal life'.

4 A Short History of Healing

The Shamans

Our remote ancestors did not by any means enjoy good health; they lived in harsh surroundings, and were weak and vulnerable compared to the beasts among whom they lived. Nomadic tribes often had to travel vast distances in search of better hunting or more fertile soil, and the weaker individuals did not survive the journeys. We know from geological findings that disease organisms existed on earth millions of years before man appeared. Java Man, whose skeleton is at least a million years old, had a diseased femur, and laboratory examination has revealed the presence of tuberculosis in an Egyptian mummy.

Because early man made no connection between his mode of life and his health, sickness was felt to be of supernatural origin and much to be feared. The Shaman or witch doctor was considered to be the only protection available against the hostile forces surrounding and governing an individual's life.

The power of the Shaman may well have originated in the veneration shown to old age in early times. Longevity was so unusual that it was thought to confer upon a man not only the wisdom of accumulated experience but also the help of his ancestors. This acceptance of wisdom in the

74

old, coupled with the honouring of bravery in the young, was the foundation for the dual system of government that existed in the early world – that of King and Priest. The hereditary chief in his youth and strength had as advisors the old-ones of his tribe. The vestiges of this system still remain in present-day society.

Gradually it became the custom for the old-ones to single out others to whom they could pass on their wisdom. They chose disciples from among the more thoughtful members of the tribe, who came to be given the special privileges of sitting with the warriors in Council and being exempt from the hazards of battle. They were consulted on all matters concerning the health and welfare of the tribe, and from them the sick learned of their ancestors' experiences under similar circumstances.

The powers of the Shaman were further increased when it was discovered that sensitivity to nature – that is to say the psychic faculty – could be heightened through fasting and vigils. By exhausting his physical strength, he developed his powers of dreaming and interpreting his dreams; as he was visited by the deceased in his sleep or trance-state, his wisdom and usefulness to the tribe grew.

With this increase in authority, so the paraphernalia surrounding the Shaman's activities was developed. As part of his ritual he wore a grotesque mask, possibly made in the likeness of the old-ones. When wearing this, he spoke with their authority. The animal mask of the Egyptian Priest may well have served the same purpose: when wearing it he assumed the power of the animal spirit which it represented. Its frightening aspect was intended to intimidate the evil spirits as well as to terrify the living spectators. The faces of the masks may well have been brought over from the dream world to express the unconscious forces locked up in the human mind.

The use of music in healing began with rattles which focused the minds of sick people on the treatment they were receiving. Early music mimicked the sounds of nature such as the cries of animals or the songs of birds. Gradually repetition of similar notes formed simple rhythms which became standardized. Sacred dances also used in healing, developed from the movements of Shamans imitating the animals whose masks they wore.

One of the earliest forms of medication was the fetish, a natural substance into which spiritual power had been induced by ritual and which then acted as a protection for the wearer. The oldest fetishes were carved from wood or bone in the likeness of a creature or sacred object. In some instances they were plants or herbs which were either chewed or boiled into a liquid, or were inserted under the skin. The original intent was to capture the spirit of the plant; gradually as certain herbs were found to be efficacious for certain conditions, so pharmacology became established.

The practices of the Shaman or witch-doctor are sometimes termed witchcraft, but this is misleading; their practices were not the perversion of a religious doctrine, but were the expression of primitive man's outlook on his world, and were therefore not necessarily evil. Because of his belief that disease was a wandering spirit, the Shaman tried to placate it and find it a new abode so that it would be willing to relinquish its victim and his village. From this practise arose the idea of a scapegoat: either someone had to be sacrificed for the good of the entire tribe, or else the spirit was inserted into a fetish which was then left outside the village precincts to be found by a stranger.

Medicine Men

In the New World, the equivalent of the European or Asian Shaman was the 'medicine man' of the Red Indians. It is important to understand that the term 'medicine' in this connection does not refer exclusively to healing by drugs or manipulation. It includes the harnessing of those forces which seem to be beyond our ordinary understanding; it means walking with the gods and knowing the ways of the spirit world.

The Medicine Man was primarily a holy man and the guardian of the secret history of the tribe. Because physical ills were attributed to the anger of one of a multitude of deities that controlled all life, propitiation for any slight to their dignity or placation of their malevolence were constantly needed. Protection against further disease was attained only through the successful appeasement of an entire hierarchy of celestial beings.

Before achieving manhood, the Indian boy of almost all tribes was expected to 'make his medicine' by retiring to some secluded spot. On a mountain peak, in a forest or on an arid plain, he fasted, prayed, mortified his flesh and meditated until he reached a state of religious fervour similar to that of the Christian ascetics. When he was thus predisposed to dreams and visions and communications from the gods, the supernatural agent guarding and directing his life would be revealed to him. Some animal or bird, some unusual conjunction of the elements, or some fantasy would become his 'medicine', to be invoked when under stress.

The Medicine Man was a very high-ranking member of the tribe who exercised four types of power: he cured the sick; he performed feats of magic; he subjected others to his will whether they were present or not; and he enlisted the help of the gods to ensure rain, abundant crops and successful hunting.

As there was no inherited priestly or ruling caste amongst the Indians, the Medicine Man was occasionally also the Chief, chosen because of the qualities he displayed. Women also belonged to this group if they were seen to be 'psychic', or if exceptional gifts or circumstances manifested in their lives. A certain Apache woman was, for instance, acknowledged to be a Medicine Man after she had survived being both mangled by a mountain lion and struck by lightning; the successful overcoming of two such disasters was felt to be an unmistakable sign.

Amongst the Hopi and Navajo tribes, certain young boys were dedicated to medical clans. Entry was obtained by apprenticeship to an established practitioner in return for a fee. The Medicine Men were often organized into societies, each one having its own distinctive secrets; the medical society of the Apaches was, for example, particularly

77

known for its spirit dances. The factors they all had in common were undoubted sincerity and pride in their profession. It was they who were in charge of all ceremonial dances; they also made the necessary preparations for hunting or war parties; they were consulted in the search for stolen property, and foretold the future; they made rain when it was needed, and conducted such ceremonies as births, marriages and burials. As a result of their undoubted importance to the tribe, they were frequently wealthy men, paid in kind with buffaloes, robes, dried meat, horses, sacks of corn or wampun. If, however, a patient's family felt that he had been neglected or badly looked after, they sometimes extracted a fine from the Medicine Man or retaliated with personal violence.

Part of the Medicine Man's effectiveness lay in his dress. Some wore masks, some wore hats, others had heavily painted faces; but whether aiming to be ridiculous or beautiful, when fully robed they presented an awesome picture.

Every male Indian of the plains tribes, and some of the forest and plateau tribes as well, had a 'medicine bag', a skin pouch containing symbolic ornaments. The skin was that of the owner's guardian animal, the legs of which had been bound with beads or quills and its nostrils filled with coloured feathers. The medicine bag always contained, amongst other items, something variously called a rhombus, bull-roarer or whizzer. The Red Indian ones were identical in form and usage with those employed by the Ancient Greeks, the Peruvians, the aboriginal New Zealanders, and the African tribes of today. It consisted of a thin piece of wood carved with symbolic figures. The most sought-after 'bull roarers' were those cut from a tree which has been struck by lightning.

Of the medical necklaces sometimes worn, the most potent ones were made from embalmed human fingers. High Wolf of the Cheyenne owned one consisting of eight left forefingers of enemy warriors whom he had killed in battle. Medical cords known as Izze cloths were worn on solemn occasions and were believed to render the owner immune to bullets and also to cure the sick. If wound around the head, they stopped headaches. Water drums were also used for healing. Made of scooped-out logs, tanned hide, or pottery, they were partially filled with water and covered by a cured skin. When rubbed with sticks, they produced a low, monotonous rumbling sound which created a hypnotic effect.

The Indian Medicine Man had at his command a wide range of substances made from plants, roots, bark and animals. Some of these produced no physical effect but had great ceremonial significance. Powdered turquoise and powdered meal, for example, were stored by the doorways of Pueblo Indians to be scattered as protection against spirits; dried willow and other leaves were smoked on certain well-established occasions. Other substances, thought to be effective as prevention or cure because they resembled the afflicting disease, were administered more as a charm than a medicine. Fetishes were used to twitch evil spirits out of a patient. When a Mohave child had whooping cough, his father abstained from drinking tea and bathed himself in the Colorado river. The Winebago attributed sickness to an unrealized desire; the Medicine Man's task was to see that desire fulfilled for the patient at whatever cost. Amongst the Hopis, a ceremonially-twisted piece of wood was placed beside a patient having convulsions, and the skin of a weasel was similarly used for a woman in labour.

A third group of substances was used by the Indians as medicines in the modern sense of the term. Their dispensing was always accompanied by prayer and chanting. They were made from herbs, always said to 'come from afar', and gathered in great secrecy at the appropriate phase of the moon. The Little Fire Fraternity of the Zuni people had, for instance, a very effective medicine for rheumatism which took four days to prepare and was made from six different substances. Gastro-intestinal disturbances were treated with willow and sage; laxatives were derived from magnesia salts found in springs and mixed with cellulose and bulk foods such as chopped bran.

Massage, hot stones and poultices were prescribed for the Indians' frequent attacks of arthritis and rheumatism. Sweat baths were also in universal use for the relief of such pain; limbs were buried for many hours at a time in hot mud.

The Indian Medicine Man was well-versed in the use of narcotics, pain-killers and intoxicants. The red bean of Texas produced delirium followed by two or three days' sleep; the sacred mushroom and the peyote bean were used as intoxicants during religious ceremonial.

Because the Indians had very little experience in dealing with contagious diseases such as measles and venereal disease, these spread like wildfire with the arrival of the white man. Sometimes no actual contact was needed. Entire Indian villages are known to have been wiped out after some Europeans had camped nearby.

The more advanced Medicine Man often had some knowledge of surgery. He could set bones, pull teeth and use a variety of surgical instruments, including one for trepanning the skull in order to lessen the pressure within and thus release unclean spirits. Wounds were sutured with hair, and infected wounds were cauterized.

The Aztec people of South America considered disease to be a punishment sent by unkind gods. Healing plants were named after various friendly gods from whom they were thought to be a gift. At the time of the Spanish conquest, three types of miracle workers existed amongst these people: the sorcerers and astrologers, and the 'Tapati' who were physicians.

In Peru the Incas had very advanced ideas about the care of the sick, whose welfare was the responsibility of the government. Primarily they treated disease through prayer and fasting, if necessary to the point of death, but skilled medical help was also available.

The tribes living in desert country used a most interesting method for protecting their young people against the constant scourge of snake bite. First a candidate was bitten by a very immature snake whose venom was still weak; then older snakes with increasingly strong venom

80

were used until the youth was able to tolerate the bite of a fully grown reptile. Thus immunization was first developed.

Most American Indian tribes believed in one God, or Great Spirit, who communicated with his children through dreams or visions. After death the soul was said to choose between dwelling in a 'happy land' or staying amongst the living to serve and protect them. The Chief Seattle declared: 'When the last Red Man shall have perished from the earth and his memory among the white man shall have become a myth, these shores will still swarm with the invisible dead of my tribe.'

The ideas taught by the Shaman or witch doctor were further developed by the Medicine Man and then integrated into a coherent system of belief. For the Shaman, most spirits were said to be evil, but to the Medicine Man many of them appeared benevolent and useful to mankind. In some parts of the continent the Medicine Men had long drawn-out battles with the wizards and witches; gradually the adherents of the black arts lost caste and were ostracized by the people.

The Medicine Man sought his god and his knowledge in the old ways through dreams, trances and visions, and most great leaders of the Indian nations from Hiawatha to Geronimo gained their strength from such visions. The renowned warrior Crazy Horse was shown in a vision that he would never be slain in battle; in effect he was killed by a government agent parleying under a flag of truce. During the Custer wars a Medicine Man was fired upon repeatedly by American soldiers from less than a hundred feet yet neither the Indian nor his horse was affected. When he returned to his own people and shook out his clothes, a number of bullets fell to the ground. He had been able to protect himself through the same conscious use of energy as demonstrated by the Hawaiian Hunas, a feat which will be explained in more detail later in this chapter.

Many of the mystical experiences recorded by the Medicine Men are very similar to those of other peoples' occult traditions, although there cannot have been any contact between them. The Red Indians saw auras, left their bodies at will to travel long distances in their spirit bodies, conversed with the dead, and used their ancestors as guides to other worlds. They understood the language of birds and animals, and could foretell events.

The fire-walking ceremony of the Californian Indians was very like the present-day rites performed in Fiji. Long trenches are built, and a fire is left burning in them for several days. After special ceremonies of purification, the firewalkers slowly pace the entire length of the trench. Occasionally one of them carries with him a piece of raw meat; by the end of the walk, the meat is burned to a crisp lump but he himself shows no sign of burning or even blistering, despite the heat in the pit reaching up to two thousand degrees fahrenheit.

Amongst the Navajo and Hopi tribes, sand pictures or dry paintings constituted an important part of healing. These traditional designs depicting the mythical history of the tribe were considered to bring special virtue to the sick, for whom they were individually made. After the ceremony they were destroyed. Such ritual has certain affinities with the methods of modern metaphysical healers who encourage the release of anxiety through art, but there is one basic and vital difference: the Medicine Man chose the forms for his patient whereas contemporary patients must find their own symbols and figures. We have become less sensitive to the power of ritual healing through becoming more individualized. But we can still benefit from overtly expressing our anxieties and fears.

Some of the Dakota tribes had a fascinating belief about the origin of their Medicine Men. It was thought that before physical birth they existed as 'flying seeds' which wafted about in the spirit world visiting various gods who instructed them in magic and medicine. Their training with the gods completed, they then journeyed all over the earth to observe the customs of different nations. Finally they chose where they wished to be born, and incarnated as Medicine Men. When their time on earth was over, they returned to the abode of the gods for further instruction. After four such cycles, their seeds returned to the space from whence they came.

When the Medicine Man went out into the night and built his lonely vigil fire on a hilltop, he placed his prayer sticks in a circle about him and smoked his medicine pipe facing towards the six directions in turn. A humble human seeking to know the ways of the gods, he made the only prayer he knew: 'Great Spirit, show us the way'.

Some echoes of Indian beliefs can be glimpsed in the teachings of the Mormons, the Church of Jesus Christ of the Latter Day Saints, which was founded by Joseph Smith. When Smith was fifteen years old, praying one night in a field on his father's farm, he had a visitation very similar to a shamanistic experience. Within a bright light which travelled down to earth were identical twin beings who told him that he would be the recipient of a true revelation. Later he was visited by a being clad in a robe of unearthly whiteness who announced himself as Moroni, 'a messenger sent from the presence of God'. Six years later, Smith was guided to unearth a stone chest which contained gold plates covered with writing in an unknown script. This Smith was taught to decipher. It was the Book of Mormon.

A similar event describing how an Eskimo woman, Uvavnuk, became a Shaman is recorded by Knud Rasmussed in his book, *Intellectual Culture of the Iglulik Eskimos*. Sitting one night outside her hut, Uvavnuk saw a glowing ball coming towards her through the moonless heavens. As it rested above her and then entered her, she saw the spirit that dwelt within the glowing ball; it had the dual form of a bear and a human. Later in the book, Rasmussed describes the case of a Caribou Eskimo to whom unknown beings spoke in his sleep. When he awoke he recalled his visions so distinctly that it soon became evident that he was destined to be a Shaman or 'Angakoq'. He was then left for several months all alone in a tiny snow hut, with scarcely any food or drink, and was ordered to think only of the Great Spirit. During such ordeals Shamans 'die a little' and this half-death qualifies them as intermediaries with the spirit world.

Egypt, Greece and Rome

By about 3000 B.C., urban life had begun in Mesopotamia, Egypt and the Indus Valley, and man himself had made a great step forward in the development of his consciousness. The 'participation mystique' through which primitive man felt himself to be primarily a member of a particular group or tribe, had begun to assume less significance, and the individual 'self-consciousness' of modern man began to take its place. As this happened, the sympathetic white magic which until now had been used for the communal good of the tribe degenerated into sorcery. Spells, potions and rituals were used to achieve personal power; the whole of society became obsessed with gods, sorcerers and demons.

By the beginning of the Mesopotamian civilization, the role of healer as practised by the Shaman or Medicine Man no longer existed, yet no recognized healers had replaced them. The sick were simply carried out into the marketplace where passers-by gave them advice based on their own experience. Later on (approximately 2000 B.C.), professional physicians came into existence. Their charges and responsibilities were carefully set out in the 'Code of Hammurabi'. Payment, which depended on the rank of the patient, was only to be made if the treatment was successful; if it had failed, the physician risked having his hand cut off.

In Egypt at this time, sick men were thought to be possessed by devils. It was rain sent by the gods as a cleansing agent which could cure them. The gods also sent signs which were to be interpreted by diviners. These omens were found in the livers of sacrificial animals and gave guidance on important decisions as well as on matters of health.

It was the Egyptian healer Imhotep who founded the tradition of healing in Temples. Many were established in his honour, and a priesthood served in their clinics. Later on, the first schools of medicine were developed at these centres.

Very little is known about the famous Greek healer Asclepius who probably lived between 1200–1000 B.C. But it was he who founded healing temples throughout the Greek States and later on in various parts of the Roman Empire. These light and airy buildings were often sited near medicinal spas. The sick who came for treatment were clothed in new white garments and put to sleep overnight on couches near the statue of Ascelpius. In his dreams the patient saw the spirit of the healer appear at his side and prescribe the appropriate remedies. In the morning the patient told the priest his dream and was treated accordingly. If no guidance was forthcoming, the process was repeated, possibly with the additional help of a drug or a hypnotic suggestion. Cures were frequent, and the walls of the temples were covered with plaques detailing the miraculous events which had taken place. Grateful patients brought offerings to the temple.

In the sixth century B.C., Greek medicine took a significant step forward with the teaching of Pythagoras, the distinguished mathematician and philosopher. Legend tells us that when his parents visited the shrine of the Pythian oracle at Delphi, the god Apollo promised them an extraordinary son; when he was born, they named him Pythagoras, which means 'mouthpiece of the Pythian oracle'.

For Pythagoras, a central fire in the universe was the prime cause of creation; it manifested everywhere and was the source of the divine spark in man. From this fire originated also all healing energy, which he termed 'pneuma'. His concept that the universe was a living being, and that physical health was closely related to psychological and spiritual well-being, was taught at his academy at Crotna, to which he attracted an enthusiastic body of students who began each day with meditation and exercises to purify the mind and strengthen the will. They studied dance, gymnastics, diet, mathematics and harmony, all of which was considered vital for the health of both body and soul. The body itself was considered as a vehicle which, through intellect and discipline, helped the soul to advance and learn its lessons.

In one of his famous 'Golden Verses', Pythagoras declared: 'Likewise know that men draw upon themselves their own misfortunes voluntarily and of their own free choice, wretches that they are! They neither see nor understand that their good is near them. There are few of them who know how to deliver themselves out of their own misfortunes. Such is the fate that binds mankind and takes away their senses. Like huge cylinders they roll to and fro always oppressed with ills without number. For fatal contention is innate in them and pursuing them everywhere tosses them up and down, nor do they perceive it. Instead of provoking and stirring it up, they ought to be yielding to avoid it.'

A century later on the Greek island of Cos, the great Hypocrates, who is honoured as the father of modern medicine, was born into a family of priest-healers. He travelled widely throughout Asia Minor and the Greek world in search of knowledge. Like Pythagoras, he believed in a healing energy which he called 'vis medicatrix naturae', the healing power of nature. The function of a physician, he taught, was to reduce or remove any impediments to the proper flow of this vital power. For him, the first law of healing was: 'Above all don't make things worse.' He advised men to 'Live a healthy life and you are not likely to fall ill except through epidemic or accident. If you do fall ill, proper regimen will give you the best chance of recovery.'

He divided individuals into four categories: sanguine, phlegmatic, choleric or melancholic. A person's disposition, he said, depended on which of the four 'Humours' or juices predominated in him: blood, phlegm, black bile or yellow bile. Health, he taught, depended on keeping these four elements in balance. Disease was often the body's attempt to re-establish a disrupted harmony, and in that sense disease was beneficial and its symptoms should not be interfered with. Nature should be allowed to work out her own cure. The healer's role was simply to ensure that nature's healing power was freely available to the patient.

Hypocrates and his followers were recognized as the first rational physicians, because they separated medicine from religion and philosophy; they advised prayer as an aid to recovery, but their emphasis was on objective therapy. They also formally established, in the famous 'Hypocratic Oath', the rules of the doctor-patient relationship which have governed the secular profession of medicine until the present day. In it are defined in detail the physician's correct approach towards his patient, his appropriate bedside manner, and his over-riding duty to heal. In no circumstances must he hasten the termination of life or condone abortion.

At the same time that Hypocrates was teaching in Greece, the healers of China were much concerned with the preparation of drugs and elixirs to prolong life. This science stemmed from the Taoist doctrine that man and nature are intermingled, and that man can discover his true powers by merging into harmony with nature. The premise that illnesses can be cured and man's life-span prolonged by natural methods rested on the conviction that each plant and herb has its own individual essence or tincture which can be extracted by chemical processes and used to support or enhance a human being's life-energy.

The cult of Asclepius was not brought to an end by the discoveries of Hypocrates, but remained for a very long time the basis of public medical practice in Greece. Even in Rome, centuries later, when a plague broke out an emissary was sent to Epidaurus to beg help from the spirit of Asclepius. Having 'allowed' himself to be taken to Rome by sea in the form of a living serpent, the 'god' slid over the side of the boat and swam to an island in the Tiber. The Romans, taking this as a sign, built a temple to Asclepius on the island and the plague abated. Several memorial tablets excavated from the site of this temple recount its miraculous cures for blindness, haemorrhages, pleurisy and other afflictions. If spiritual healing could produce cures such as these, it is understandable that such respect should continue to be given to the old god and his priests. When the new secular doctors, for all their learning, severed their connection with the mystical institutions of healing, did they not lose much of the insight into the origin, meaning, and treatment of disease possessed by the initiated priest-physicians of the classical world?

By the end of the first century A.D. Greek doctors, followers of Hypocrates, had established themselves in Rome and were notorious for their profitable practices. The famous orator, Cato, condemned them roundly, declaring that Rome had flourished without doctors for six centuries only to be murdered in the end by Greek physicians. Pliny considered that a physician was the only person who could kill someone with sovereign impunity.

The most famous of these Greek doctors practicing in Rome was Galen, who was born in 131 A.D. in Mysia. He did much research on the anatomy of animals but had no opportunity to study human bodies as this was prohibited by the authorities. He followed Hypocrates' system of the four humours and sought to correct imbalances with medicines of sympathy and antipathy. He put much faith in amulets, and was the originator of the anodyne necklace.

The Essenes

It is through the discovery and deciphering of the Dead Sea Scrolls, their Holy Books, that we have learned about the Jewish sect known as the Essene Brotherhood. Living in a community beside the Dead Sea, they flourished in the three centuries before Christ, and became the forerunners and supporters of the Christian religion. They themselves faded out in about 100 A.D. when their work with the new religion was complete.

The Essenes' secret initiatory rites were similar to those practised at Eleusis in Greece, and conditions for acceptance in the Order were very strict. A novice was required to wait a full year before joining the Order, and his suitability was confirmed only after a further two years. The Brethren taught a life of strict purity, both moral and religious. They considered the killing of animals for food to be unlawful, and they understood the occult virtues of plants and minerals.

Each day at dawn they meditated on one of the seven angels of the earth, the trees and the minerals, and as they gardened and farmed they consciously co-operated with these forces. At noon they practised Contemplation of the Sevenfold Peace, seeing peace and harmony as the dynamic forces to which they could attune themselves in order to influence their relationships with other individuals, with mankind, and with the Heavenly Father. At night they meditated on the Angelic Beings, drawing through them on the cosmic oceans of wisdom, love and power. These angelic beings they described as working always for harmony in conformity with the divine law.

Having recognized the importance of alternating their time between physical labour and revivifying periods of communion with their Earthly Mother and Heavenly Father, the Essenes led long and healthy lives, with a life-span of up to 120 years.

The Druids

In the west of Europe, the teachings of the Druids were beginning to influence European thinking. These priests of the Celtic nations have been much maligned by Roman writers who stressed almost exclusively the fact that they practised human sacrifices. This misrepresentation of Druidic rites was used as an excuse by the Roman conquerors for suppressing these powerful opponents to their rule.

Centres of learning were established all over western Europe by the Druids. They usually taught in woodland groves and only by word of mouth. Crowds of sick people attended these teaching centres, and healing miracles were frequent.

The Druids saw themselves as stewards of the Earth Mother. Their ceremonies were performed for the purpose of establishing a flow of energy between the world of spirit and the physical world. The earth was recognized as a living being on which there existed certain sacred power centres; through these the cosmic energies could flow to earth, especially at the four Festivals of the Equinoxes and the Solstices. They considered it their appointed task to keep open these channels at sacred centres such as Glastonbury and Stonehenge.

Because they believed that every religion was, of necessity, a science of human regeneration concealed beneath mystical symbols, they were able to accept the teaching of Jesus as soon as they were told of Him by the early Christian missionaries.

A belief in reincarnation was central to Druid teaching. Many lifetimes of learning were considered necessary for the understanding of the divine laws. So certain were they of incarnating again, that they were prepared to grant loans to be repaid in a future life. Records of such transactions still exist in the British Museum.

At a later stage, when Roman persecution had driven all Druid ceremony and teaching underground, their Gorsedd circle became the Round Table of the Arthurian stories, and Druid knowledge was preserved and spread through the songs and stories of Medieval Europe.

Dark Ages

We know very little of the history of Europe during the Dark Ages that followed the fall of Rome but, our knowledge of life in Anglo-Saxon England suggests that hardly anyone could expect to live a long or healthy life. Graveyards of this period contain few remains of people over forty-five years old, and there is a large percentage of infants and young children. Mortality was highest when storms destroyed crops or when disease killed off cattle. Most skeletons provide evidence of rickets, tuberculosis and arthritis.

Europe's hostile climate bound people into social and economic codes, in which loyalty to the local lord and to one's kin were paramount. These codes of behaviour led to constant conflict, which in turn spread famine and epidemics. It would appear that the pestilence which followed the Viking invasion killed more people than the actual fighting. Earlier pestilence at Jarrow in Northern England reduced the number of monks to only two: the Abbot and a young monk called Bede. There was even a near relapse into paganism during the five years after the Synod of Whitby, due to the untimely death of most of the clergy.

These epidemics continued intermittently until the end of the Middle Ages, encouraged by lack of personal hygiene and the filthy state of the villages. Medicine was primitive among these people. Sickness was 'bad' and to be counteracted by the application of 'good'. Disease, like war, was seen as a just punishment for sin. Churchmen advocated repentance and treated illness with Blessings and holy relics. Some herbal knowledge survived from earlier times but in mutilated form and faultily transcribed. Many prescriptions of the period carry the postscript: 'With God's help no harm will come.' There was much reliance on the magic number three: medication was given three times a day, or 'nine times if the need is great'. Colours were felt to be significant: yellow was a cure for jaundice; the rust from church bells cured 'the flux'; peony root was given for insanity, and the pink eyes taken from a live crab would cure 'swollen eyes'.

Churchmen and monks tended the sick as part of their duties but they were not allowed to shed blood, so laymen were needed for minor surgery and for blood-letting which was highly esteemed as a cure. 'Evil humours' were treated by leeches drawing blood from the appropriate site, since blood was believed to be stationary within the body. It was said to be dangerous to let blood on the fourth day of the moon, but springtime was considered to be very propitious for this purpose.

In the Dark Ages these monasteries were the only schools and the monks were the only people who could read and write. It was they who kept records of the classic texts on medicine, mathematics and other subjects and it was from the monasteries, especially those of the Benedictine Order, that the great Universities of Europe gradually developed. Supported by both Church and State,

91

they taught the works of Galen and Avicenna; but no research was carried out, nor was any attempt made to improve the general health of the people.

The Middle Ages

European life in the Middle Ages was overshadowed by the devil and all his works. A demon lurked in every dark corner, and no man was safe, even in church where wooden carvings of imps were often placed under the pews as a warning. Belief in the evil machinations of a personal devil was taught from church pulpits, to explain such natural calamities as the plague and crop failure and to condemn as witches those people gifted with psychic abilities who were said to be in league with the 'evil one'. Even manifestations of joy and gaiety were frowned upon by the church as expressions of the devil's influence, thus creating neuroses which no one knew how to combat.

The era of witchcraft brought fear and misery to whole populations, and death to many thousands of helpless people. Because men learned to so fear their neighbours, mass hysteria brought about the almost complete demoralization of spiritual life. Medicine at this time, such as it was, was available to the rich, but poor people depended on the herbs and charms of the local 'wise woman', who always lived just outside the village limits. These herbalists sometimes became widely regarded, and persons of consequence were led to consult them. The inevitable outcome of such fame was denunciation as a witch, either by a personal enemy or by a nearby doctor who saw his livelihood threatened. It was enough to report the alleged offender to the Ecclesiastical Courts; boxes for receiving anonymous accusations were conveniently placed outside churches. It is not surprising that many such accusations stemmed from animosity, greed, jealousy or a desire for revenge.

During this period, even the orthodox medical profession was very much at risk. Training in the Universities was so inadequate that many keen doctors continued their education by travelling the countryside consulting local herbalists. They even risked life and limb to reach Spain and other countries where the advanced Moorish medicine was taught. But when such doctors returned to practise in Europe, they faced danger on two fronts: if their cures were too successful they might well be denounced to the Inquisition, or they could be accused of malpractise by their envious colleagues. There are also several cases on record of doctors growing their own herbs instead of employing the local apothocary; the latter then incited local people against them and they were forced to flee the town.

By the end of the fourteenth century, belief in the all-pervasiveness of the devil and his works had lost some ground, although remnants of it still persisted. When the physicians of a certain town decided that a local swamp was the cause of an epidemic, and the local clergy were equally certain that Satan was to blame, compromise was reached by the physicians concluding that the swamp was the direct cause of the fever but that the devil was the cause of the swamp!

Paracelsus

The revival of classical learning in medicine was marked in the early fifteenth century by the burning of the books of Galen and Avicenna. This took place in a public ceremony at Basle University, led by a Swiss doctor, Paracelsus, who had studied medicine with Moslem physicians in Constantinople. Although uncouth and ill-mannered, he was undoubtedly one of the greatest physicians Europe has ever produced. He had studied the healing practices of gypsies, witches, herbalists and alchemists; he was interested in magnetism and was learned in the Mysteries of the Jewish Qabalah. Convinced that all means, both physical and magical, were acceptable if they contributed to the patient's health, he combined, with strange results, the talents of a seer and those of a doctor. Paracelsus wrote in German rather than in the conventional Latin because he considered it far more important to be clearly understood than to be academically impressive.

Paracelsus was the one bright spot in the gloomy picture of medicine during his age. This extraordinary man, weaving together the mysticism of Pythagoras and the rational thinking of Hypocrates with a genius of his own, contributed enormously to the understanding of diseases such as syphilis, silicosis and goitre. He also gained much new knowledge about the healing of wounds. Although homeopathy did not yet exist in his time, he was an early advocate of this therapy, for he considered that if given in small doses, 'What makes ill a man also cures him.'

Jung wrote of him: 'We see in Paracelsus not only a pioneer in the domains of chemical medicine but also in those of an empirical, psychological healing science.'

Paracelsus deemed man to have three bodies: first the animal body which houses our lower instincts, then a star or astral body which contains our understanding of art, wisdom and the higher instincts, and thirdly a body consisting solely of an immortal spark of energy. The first two bodies are part of mortal man and therefore subject to disease; the third, being part of God, is not. He taught that a healing energy radiates within and around man like a luminous sphere. This energy, which he termed 'archaeus', can operate at a distance to both cause and cure disease. Although the archaeus motivates the physical body and is the source of its energy, it can be influenced by the mind: negative thought can block its flow and give rise to disease. He taught that resolute imagination can accomplish all things, and that one gains knowledge through both intuition and experience. To neglect either method, he said, is a recipe for disaster. Intuitive reason, guided by archaeus, is the all-pervading force with which one should be actively co-operating. He considered that 'a physician should be the servant of nature not her enemy, he should be able to guide and direct her in her struggle for life and not throw, by his unreasonable influence, fresh obstacles in the way of recovery.'

Paracelsus believed that all bodies have their roots in the atmosphere. He envisaged the universe as an inverted garden, in which air is the source of all elements and substances necessary for maintaining the living processes. Air is also the source of intelligence and of emotion and of the patterns by which living species are differentiated. Man's uniqueness lies, for him, in the fact that he contains within himself diverse magnetic poles able to attract countless forms of energy. Thus man is capable of knowing everything necessary to his own survival. The roots and seeds of universal achievement lie within him. He responds, however, *only* to those energies which resonate with his own understanding. For example, an individual will never energize an emotional power which is inconsistent with the development of his own emotional nature: if he hates, he cannot utilize the archetype of love – unless of course he changes his own nature. Man exists, said Paracelsus, in the midst of forces which are beyond his conscious understanding, yet gradually, through the development of his own mind, he attains true learning and becomes responsive to the universal energies which sustain learning and help it to increase.

Paracelsus wrote: 'Medicine is not merely a science but an art; it does not consist in compounding pills and plasters and drugs of all kinds but it deals with the processes of life which must be understood before they can be guided. A powerful will may cure where a doubt will end in failure. The character of the physician may act more powerfully on the patient than all the drugs employed.'

Contemporaries of Paracelsus claimed to have seen him dancing in his garden and communing with spirits as he gathered dew for his medical concoctions. His enemies considered that he owed his successes to a pact made with the devil, but his grateful patients were delighted with the results of his ministrations. Almost inevitably, considering the period in which he lived, the powers of darkness proved too strong for even such a multi-talented man. He was murdered in 1541 by professional assassins hired by jealous rivals.

The revival of learning in the sixteenth century brought with it many advances in medicine. Leonardo da Vinci studied the human form closely, particularly its bones and muscles, and although he did not himself publish his drawings, his influence was paramount in the first textbook of anatomy wholly based on direct observation of the body. This was printed in Basle in 1543. The resulting improvement in knowledge was a great help to military surgeons during the prolonged Wars of Religion.

The seventeenth century saw two great advances in medical skills: William Harvey demonstrated the circulation of the blood, and Galileo produced the first effective microscope as a by-product of inventing the telescope. These two discoveries were of inestimable value in the development of modern medicine and its new philosophical attitude, as can be gauged from a book by Thomas Sydenham published in 1666, *Methodus Curandi Febres*, which begins as follows: 'A disease, in my opinion, how prejudicial soever its cause may be to the body, is no more than a vigorous effort of Nature to destroy the morbid matter and thus recover the patient.'

The Industrial Revolution of the eighteenth century resulted in a mass exodus of country people into the towns, and made attention to Public Health an urgent necessity. By the end of the century towns were lighted, streets were paved, drains covered and sewers improved; nevertheless a constant supply of pure water was not available until the following century, and health conditions in towns were deplorable.

The prosperity brought to Britain by the new industries gave rise to the development of spas. The mineral waters available at Bath, Leamington and many other towns had long been recognized as having healing properties. Considered to be Holy Wells, and much revered, they had sadly degenerated after the Reformation into 'wishing wells'. But by the end of the seventeenth century they had again become places of healing. Bath was the most highly regarded of these spas since its springs maintained a constant temperature of 120 degrees. By 1704 a Pump Room had been built to accommodate the fashionable visitors who came to immerse their bodies in the waters for lengthy periods, with scant regard for basic hygiene. These baths continued in favour throughout the whole of the eighteenth century.

Much unorthodox medicine was practised during this period and rejuvenating remedies were provided at great cost. These ranged from tinctures of gold, vegetable infusions, oil distilled from stags' horns, and flesh of viper, to the grim expedient of drinking young children's blood. This latter practice was fortunately made illegal both in England and in France.

Royal Sovereigns were said to have the inherited ability to cure, through their touch, the 'King's Evil' (scrofula). This practice continued in England until the coming of the Hanoverian Kings. In France, Louis XV ministered to two thousand sick people at his Coronation.

By the nineteenth century, the theory of germs as a basis for many diseases became generally accepted; bacteriology was developed into a science; many advances were made in paediatrics, chemotherapy and blood transfusions. Vitamin deficiency was studied, and improvements were made in the treatment of the insane.

The twentieth century has witnessed success in the specific treatment of certain illnesses, and much new insight has been gained in psychology. The discovery of anti-biotics has undoubtedly been a great contribution to the conquest of disease.

The Hunas

As Western medicine has gradually become more and more specialized, its 'holistic' aspect – consideration of the whole man and his needs rather than his specific symptoms or diseases – has been largely neglected. It is this view of man, however, that the Hunas have always held.

When William Ruft Brigham settled in Hawaii at the end of the last century as Curator of the Museum, the ancient healing knowledge of the Hawaiians still existed amongst

97

their Kahunas or priests who, although outlawed as black magicians by the missionaries, continued to work amongst the local people. The word Kahuna means 'keeper of the secret', and although Westerners found it very difficult to learn anything about the Kahunas' methods, their abilities were amply demonstrated. They could walk over hot lava flows, make effective 'death prayers', and in some cases could even bring about instant healing of crushed bones. Dr Brigham was himself able to fire-walk under the protection of the Kahunas, but to the end of his long life he was no nearer to understanding their system. It was Max Freedom Long and his associates who continued his studies and discovered that the Hunas' secret is contained within the Hawaiian language itself.

The Polynesian people now living in Hawaii came to the Pacific Islands at about the time of Christ. From where had they come? Legend suggests that their wisdom originated in the lost continent of Atlantis. When it was destroyed, some of its survivors travelled via North Africa to ancient Egypt. Although there are no written records of this, traces of the Huna systems have been found in the Egypt of the Pyramid builders. From there a small body of Kahunas and their followers went to the Atlas Mountains in North Africa, where their teaching flourished until New Testament days, while the main body of their people journeyed through India and Asia to the Pacific Islands, where their teaching could be practised without interference from any established priesthood. There it continued undisturbed until the arrival of the Christian missionaries.

Central to the Huna teaching is the concept that man consists of three separate selves. The low Self, which is at a primitive, almost animal, stage of development, corresponds roughly to the Freudian unconscious. Although able to remember, it cannot reason; it controls our appetites and desires; it can be trained to serve the needs of the middle Self; and it is in touch with the elemental world and with the Collective Unconscious of the human race. Situated in the solar plexus, it is the repository for the 'mana' or life force which it can supply to the other Selves.

The middle Self is the 'I' of personal consciousness. This Self cannot remember, but has full reasoning powers and is situated in the left hemisphere of the brain.

The Higher Self is a guardian angel or Overself. It knows the past, the present, and as much of the future as has already been planned. It is contained in the right hemisphere of the brain and is a Father-Mother spirit over-lighting our lives.

All things are believed by the Hunas to have a shadow or etheric body. The etheric body of the Low Self, although invisible, is dense and sticky, and from it invisible bonds connect us to everything and everyone with whom we come into contact. These cords are called 'aka' threads and can stretch without breaking through time and space. The etheric bodies of our other two Selves do not emit these threads.

Kahuna magic works by teaching the three Selves to manipulate the energy or 'mana' of their three etheric bodies. The principal difficulty here is that the three Selves must be acting in perfect harmony with one another. Our Middle Self cannot communicate directly with either the Higher Self or the Lower Self; it can, however, be contacted by the Lower Self during dreams, while under hypnosis, or through the use of a pendulum. In order for the magic to be effective, the Middle Self must in one of these ways receive notification that the Higher and Lower Selves wish to communicate, and the Middle Self must temporarily allow itself to be bypassed. If the Self centred in the solar plexus is to 'talk with' the Self in the right hemisphere of the brain in order to create magic, the activity of the right hemisphere must be increased and intensified by an additional supply of mana energy. The ability to transmit mana from the Lower Self to the Higher Self constitutes the main training of a Kahuna.

In order instantly to mend a broken bone or remove a cancerous growth, the High Self must learn to dissolve the injured or diseased tissues and bone into their original ectoplasm and then re-solidify them into their healthy form. As the etheric body of the Low Self is a perfect replica of the entire physical body, it is this etheric body which provides the ectoplasm with a mould in which it can solidify. This process of dematerialization and rematerialization requires an immense amount of energy, called 'mana loa'.

Although belonging to the same body, the three Selves are totally independant of each other; if they become separated, mental illness results. It is interesting that the Kahunas were aware of complexes and schizophrenia long before Freud and Jung were born.

Huna magic was nearly always used for healing. To harm another person was the only sin recognized by the Hunas. However, the death prayer was occasionally used by a Kahuna. The ghostly subconscious of a dead person was charged with 'mana' and sent in search of its victim, who was identified by means of a strand of hair or nail-paring which the Kahuna had previously obtained. The spirit then entered the victim, curled up inside him, and then gradually straightened out, absorbing all his 'mana' as he did so. Death within three days was certain. The process was always the same: a numbness started at the feet and eventually made its way to the heart.

The Hawaiian language used relatively simple words to convey complex ideas, for example the word 'to worship' was 'hoo mana', meaning that to worship was first to generate an extra supply of 'mana', or low-voltage vital force, then to make contact with the Higher Self, to form the thought of prayer and finally, by stepping up the voltage of the vital force, materialize the prayer into fact.

Conclusion

As modern, scientific knowledge has developed, primitive healing techniques have been increasingly scorned. At the same time primitive medicine itself seems in some cases to have degenerated, losing touch with its spiritual sources. Without this contact, the techniques immediately become less successful than 'orthodox' medicine. But now Western medicine is suffering from such prolonged neglect of the spiritual aspect of life that it is not as effective an instrument as it should be. Perhaps the time has now come to re-examine the practices and wisdom of other cultures, past and present, and study the belief systems that lie behind them. We may well be at the beginning of a Renaissance in healing which will have as profound an effect on our future well-being as the cultural Renaissance had on our intellectual outlook.

5 Some Practical Aspects of Healing

Now that we have looked at healing through the eyes of medicine and the Church, and have been given a short history of how healing was practised in other countries at other times, we will turn to the more practical aspects of the subject seen from the point of view of a lay healer.

The Dissolving Barrier

It is both sad and uncreative that such strong barriers have existed, for many reasons and for many years, between orthodox medicine and healing. As we have seen in our first two chapters, both groups have been much impoverished by this rift. Above all the patient has suffered. He has been forced to choose between the two ways of treating disease (even the expression 'alternative medicine' has promoted this sense of choice), when a combination of the two could well produce the best results.

Why should this choice be forced upon him? Why should a patient have to refuse any help that can reasonably be given? Why should his doctor make him feel guilty because he has been to a herbalist or a radionics practitioner? And why, equally, should a healer try to cut him off from medical and surgical assistance as if to make him prove his commitment to healing? Surely such a situation can only cause destructive anxiety to the patient who feels that whichever choice he makes may lessen his chances of a cure. And if he does decide to pursue two therapies simultaneously and feels that he cannot divulge this fact to either practitioner, surely greater harm could be done to his health than could ever be done to the self-esteem of either doctor or healer.

However deep the fundamental issues which divide orthodoxy and healing, it is to be hoped that everything possible will be done by both sides to further the improvement in relationship which is gradually occurring. Barriers between the two groups *are* weakening, and at increasing speed. In the last ten years, for instance, healers have been authorized to visit patients in most hospitals. At times their reception by the staff is not warm, and their conditions of work uncongenial, but at least they are officially allowed to be there. There are now even healers on call to many hospitals for any patients who require their services.

As unofficially as possible, and usually after conventional methods have failed, a few doctors are now beginning to send their patients to a chiropractor, an osteopath or an acupuncturist whom they consider to be absolutely reliable. There are also small groups starting up, most of them informally, in which orthodox men are joining with various complementary therapists to treat their patients in any way that seems appropriate and helpful. An increasing number of doctors are also allowing healers to consult them for advice on technical matters.

Another hopeful sign is the increasing number of lectures and conferences at which scientists, doctors and healers are not only meeting for discussion, but are speaking from the same platform. The promotion of this rapprochement has been done in large part by the Wrekin Trust and the Scientific and Medical Network, but a growing number of groups and movements, many of them primarily concerned with cancer, are hastening the process.

103

There are of course still many many doctors to whom the mention of healers is an anathema, and nothing seems to penetrate their determination to disregard the whole subject. Any improvement in a patient's condition attributed to a healer is immediately classified as a 'spontaneous remission' or as part of the normal course of the illness. All healings are dismissed as non-verifiable; lack of documentation or a questionable diagnosis are given as reasons for not using them as scientific evidence. By labelling a disease 'psychosomatic', they so belittle its status that its 'cure' is said to mean only that it never really existed in the first place.

On the whole, the medical profession still views with gravest dismay the activities of people who are often without scientific training, and who must rely largely on their intuitive powers to diagnose and heal. This attitude is in many ways understandable. Doctors, who have spent long years studying their profession, find it outrageous that untrained laymen should profess to understand anything about illness.

But here science itself is, most interestingly, coming to the defence of the healer. The experiments of biologists and physicists of the most impeccable reputation are beginning to assure the medical profession that healers' claims are not entirely fanciful. Energy fields do exist; paranormal powers can be proven in laboratories; there *is* far more to the world than our five senses and rational minds can explain. And these facts, even if at this stage not totally understood or accepted by all doctors, are nevertheless influencing them. Many beliefs once unquestioned are no longer so cut and dried. There are still barriers between the two fields, but at least some conversation is taking place over or through them.

One of the most significant chinks in the barrier has actually been made by the public because of its growing disquiet about the use of drugs. The era of euphoria, when it was thought that drugs would be discovered to cure all ills, has now been outgrown. We must do more for our well-being than just sit back and swallow pills. Nearly

104

everyone has now become aware of the dangers from drugs whose side-effects are sometimes worse than the original suffering. The thalidomide case dramatically highlighted a situation which occurs continually – although less violently and with less publicity. As the rate of drug-induced diseases increases (seventeen per cent of all patients in hospital are suffering from the ill effects *caused* by a medicine), surely we must become more open to the idea of natural therapies which either can help us or at least will not harm us.

The second factor, which should contribute considerably to a better relationship between medicine and healing in the near future, is the work being done by the College of Healing. They are attempting to devise acceptable verifiable standards for those complementary therapies for which no set qualifications so far exist. Until now, assessments of a healer's effectiveness have been based only on reputation and alleged results. There are too many subjective elements in such a judgment for it to be acceptable to trained scientists. But once an objective criterion has been established for healers, medical men who want to start bridging the divide can be assured that the healer they choose conforms to a certain level of proficiency.

A third hopeful sign is the new, sober note being sounded by most healers. It is far more acceptable to rationally-oriented people such as doctors than was the old-style 'mystique'. As healers become more numerous and more accepted, they are losing the need to make an impact and to prove themselves. The mystery and theatricals with which some of them surrounded their work are no longer appropriate to the current mood and are gradually disappearing. So are the large healing demonstrations of the past which were once the only way to attract the attention and interest of the public. This is of long-term benefit to the healing movement because the hysteria sometimes generated at these meetings, and at certain Church Healing Services, is very detrimental to the reputation of healing; and the results obtained at them are only too easily dismissed by doctors. As this new sobriety increases and information about healing is disseminated in a serious way, and as healers become more willing to have their work scientifically tested and recorded, doctors will begin to recognize in them a shared devotion and dedication, even though their training and talents are so entirely different.

There is another, more subtle, factor which should be mentioned here: the cultural climate of the 80s, which is conducive to the co-operation for which we are hoping. The new generation is more in tune with the paranormal and the intuitive, with meditation and receptivity, than were their parents. And healing fits easily into this type of thought-patterns. Whether consciously or not, and however slowly, these influences are breaking down iron orthodoxy.

How Long does Healing Take?

One of the first questions people ask about healing is how long it takes. The answer ranges from instant success to definitive failure. Because the power of healing is limitless, a total, instantaneous healing is neither more unlikely nor of a fundamentally different quality than a partial, slow one. But the time must be right, and though instant cures certainly do occur, to expect one – especially if the disease is congenital or of long standing – would be unreasonable and could lead to disappointment.

Normally a patient should expect to make several visits to a healer, especially if his or her body has become accustomed to its disease and must be weaned away from it. The speed of the recovery and the profundity of its effect will very much depend on the patient's behaviour and attitude of mind between treatments and after the course has ended. If he is determined to get better and follows the healer's practical advice, he will break up the patterns that made him ill. Whether these were simple violations to his body, such as the use of alcohol and drugs or chronic insufficient sleep, or whether they were more subtly

106

disguised as destructive thought, distorted values or repressed emotions, they would all have one factor in common: his true self would recognize them as being dangerous to him and would not be really surprised that their wrongness manifest as disease.

A person who is cured instantly and *remains* free of his disease is probably someone who has already prepared the way for the healer by gaining insight into his own state of mind. By understanding what has generated that particular disease, he will have become ripe to shed it, and the healer will simply provide the impulse that shifts him into his next stage of development.

If, on the other hand, the patient's body is instantly cured but his psyche and spirit have not been able to keep pace with the cure, the behaviour and thought patterns which first caused the disease will still be in charge and will inevitably regain their dominance. At this point it is of paramount importance that a patient receive a clear explanation of what is happening to him, so that he is not disheartened and can help the healer regain, at a slower pace, the ground which was too quickly covered. Having once experienced the reality of no longer having to accommodate his disease, the patient will be in a far stronger position; its hold on him will have been weakened. If further healing is then given, progress will be more easily made than if the instant healing had never taken place. Having been dramatically ejected from his rut of ill-health, the patient must not be allowed to waste the confidence this should have given him. Nor, incidentally, should the healer falter at this point. Although something more is clearly needed, the missing elements are well worth pursuing.

One of the grave dangers of mass healing sessions has been the absence of this kind of follow-up. Where there was either improvement or total cure which then regressed, the patient urgently needed someone to help him consolidate the original healing. If there was no one available, he very naturally felt desperately discouraged and let down.

107

The Need for Disease

At one end of the spectrum are the patients whose body, psyche and spirit are entirely, instantly and permanently affected by healing; at the other end are those who derive no benefit from it whatsoever. There are several possible reasons for this which will be discussed in a later chapter, but one of them is particularly relevant here as it so much affects the relationship between a healer and his patient. There would seem to be certain conditions of ill-health which are not yet *ready* to be cured. The patient still *needs* them. In these circumstances the healer should direct all his power to helping the patient understand the reason for this need. Understanding a need is the only effective way to resolve it.

One possible explanation for a person's still being locked into some subtle relationship with his disease is given by those religions where reincarnation and Karma are basic hypotheses. There it is recognized that the law of Cause and Effect is inescapable. The Karma that has been created by an individual's behaviour must be paid for in this life or a future life until he reaches a state of perfection and can be liberated from the necessity of returning to earth. If then his present disease has been caused by his own behaviour, whether in this life or in past lives, he must live out the full lesson which the disease is teaching him. If it does not respond any better to healing than to orthodox treatment, it may well be a Karmic disease which he is not yet able to shed.

As well as teaching us lessons we need to learn, illnesses are often given us as the means by which we can redeem a hurt we have inflicted on someone. If that full redemption had not yet taken place, the healer could not release the patient from his disease, he could only help him become aware of what still remained to be done.

Whether or not this particular explanation is acceptable to us, we could probably all agree that gaining self-knowledge is one of the most healing of all processes. We should therefore take full note of our illnesses and learn to decipher their messages instead of deadening their symptoms with pain-killers and other drugs. Some of these messages are clear-cut: if our eyes or ears, for instance, are not functioning well, it is likely that we are excluding something that we should be seeing or hearing. Other signals from our bodies can be more subtle and need more interpretation. If our joints are becoming stiff and our movements ponderous, is it only our body that is finding motion difficult? Or do the hard physical particles arresting our joints symbolize the state of our minds and psyches? Have we stopped growing? Are we no longer flexible and open to new ideas or emotions? Can nothing any longer transform and enrich us? Translating your own signals will almost certainly be painful, but it will also be most rewarding, if for no other reason than the physical benefit you will derive from it.

Cases Where Cure is Difficult

The question of whether all diseases are equally susceptible to healing is a difficult one, because the rules governing it are not those to which we have been accustomed in allopathic medicine. Healing works more like homeopathy in that it treats the person rather than the disease. If a condition will not be cured and it is not a case of Karmic disease as discussed above, it may be that the person does not *want* to be cured. His illness may, for instance, guarantee him receiving care and attention that would never come his way if he were healthy. Or, more practically, ill-health may assure him a pension.

Certain illnesses, of which multiple sclerosis is one, could be considered harder to help than most others. But if illness is seen as the product of a patient's life, or past lives, rather than as an arbitrary visitation from outside, it will be understood that there must be a common denominator amongst the people who 'get' multiple sclerosis, and that it is this factor which is the difficult thing to cure. What makes this group of people vulnerable to these crippling diseases in the same way that another group with different problems produces illnesses like alcoholism or drug addiction? Are these people who, perhaps unconsciously, deep inside themselves, are refusing to participate in life; with the help of the multiple sclerosis are they slowly closing down the activity of their bodies? To reverse such a deeply sad and negative process is very difficult indeed, but it cannot even be started until the healer can help the patient become aware of what he is doing to himself.

The Healer-Patient Relationship

Whatever outward form the disease has taken, it should not be seen as a free-standing malevolent creature to be attacked, but as an integral part of the patient which must be first understood and then absorbed into his consciousness. Only in this way will the disease not recur. The more the patient can visualize himself as a healthy entirety, the more he can allow access to the healing energies, the faster will be his recovery. He should also be encouraged in every possible way to change the disease-forming patterns of his daily life.

A sensitive healer should be very aware of his patient's background and should try his best not to say anything or demand anything that could shock his susceptibilities. This may sound difficult if the two of them first meet in the neutral surroundings of a healing room; yet most people send out considerable information about themselves through their speech, clothes, and movements, and a healer should respond to these messages. If he is not careful and makes assumptions which it is impossible for the patient to accept, the opportunity to help him will have been lost.

All the patient's education and belief system should be fully and intelligently used. The patient should be encouraged to *participate* in his healing and to take as much responsibility for his own life as he is able. If he is not yet ready to take any, the healer should also recognize this and not expect it of him.

The question of whether healers should accept money from their patients is a thorny one. Some healers claim that receiving payment for a natural gift endangers the gift itself.

They feel that it should be freely used for others. This is a very generous attitude, but if someone wants to make full use of his talent and has no other source of income, he must surely accept some form of payment in order to free his mind from practical matters. The fact that he has no specialized training or expensive equipment is irrelevant to the argument. He is giving of his time and love, and a labourer is worthy of his hire. There is, besides, another very important consideration: people value more deeply something for which they have paid. They tend to consider an unpaid healer as an amateur. Conditioned as we are to buy what we need and want, we take more seriously the instructions given to us by someone to whom we have paid a fee, *however* small. The fee somehow seals a bargain. It is also a very healthy expression of thanks for what has already been done. A compromise which can perhaps satisfy both protagonists in the discussion is that the healer should accept only that which he *needs* either to cover expenses or to fulfill his responsibilities. It is probably only when someone tries to make a profit from a gift such as healing that there is the danger of destroying that gift.

Finding a Healer

From a practical point of view, finding a sound healer is not always easy. A personal recommendation is the best, because your friend should know whether you and the healer are likely to be compatible. If at present you do not know anyone who goes to a healer, you may well find that the very fact of your wanting to contact one will attract to you the information you need. Should you find that you do not get on well with the first person you visit and you have the opportunity to try someone else, do so. Certain healers are undoubtedly better suited to certain patients. It is also probably true, except in rare cases, that certain healers achieve greater success with certain diseases. This statement does not contradict the fundamental fact that it is the patient, not the disease, that is being treated. But the healer will inevitably have his own affinities and interests;

111

he may also have had more experience with particular categories of illness. His personality must also affect his relationship with the patient, at least during their interview. While the healing itself is taking place, however, he will be entirely divorced from his everyday self – so try not to be put off if you do not like him personally, but concentrate on the fact that he is a good healer. Despite their specialized gift of channelling energy, remember that healers are still ordinary people coping with their own defects.

As long as a healer's *intention* is good, you need not worry that he will harm you. As a channel for the creative power, which is always seeking to restore balance and harmony, he can at worst be such an ineffective channel that no energy reaches you through him.

First Visit to a Healer

When someone first goes to a healer, he is not really sure what to expect, and probably has no touchstone by which to judge what he finds. Let us start then with what a healer should *not* do.

He should not make wild promises. No healer, however experienced, can predict the exact results of his treatment. He can sometimes tell from experience and intuition what is probable, and whether or not it is worth the patient continuing the treatment. He will know whether good contact has been established, and how deeply the patient responded. But he should not make specific assurances of cure because it is not he who is in charge of the healing; he is only the channel for the healing energy and no more can be achieved than what is *right* for the patient. A euphoric approach is often generated by a touching enthusiasm for everything connected with healing, but it can also be very dangerous, because if the promises prove groundless, or even only partially realizable, the patient is worse off than before. Damage has also been done to the whole healing movement.

Another warning signal is if a healer tries to modify your

entire life style. Again, his actions may stem from the best and most sincere motives, but take it easy. The most effective and deep changes are brought about slowly, with the full participation of the patient, so change your diet gradually, meditate for only short periods of time at first etc. And if you do not fancy any New Age activities or thinking, then leave them. You may come to them later on; you may not. Don't let anyone else try to decide for you. There is only one essential in order for healing to be as successful as possible: be responsive. Allow love and goodwill to flow from the healer deep into your being.

A good healer has no need to boost his ego with extravagant claims, nor to act as though healing is in any way mysterious or exotic. The more straightforward and balanced he appears to you, the better he is likely to be at his job.

6 Self-healing

Self-healing requires a greater amount of inner peace and self-awareness than healing someone else, because you have to fulfil two roles simultaneously. Despite your own pain or suffering, you must contact your still centre, channel the healing energy, and then absorb it. This demands a detachment which is difficult to achieve. It is, however, the basis of all 'visualization' techniques which are of the greatest importance in combatting serious diseases such as cancer.

Visualization Techniques

This method teaches the patient to visualize, as vividly as possible, the organisms which are attacking him, and then to re-absorb them into his body where they can be accommodated by all that is still healthy in him. Because they are a part of him, however undesirable, they must not be angrily rejected, or, in most cases, separated from him by surgery. Being the products of the negative, unloving sides of his character, they must be recognized and then transformed into something healthy. Unless they are, the disease will inevitably return.

Thought forms have enormous power, and those which

are built of violence, resentment, bitterness, and anger lie like unexploded bombs within our bodies until such time as we can gently dismember them, objectively examine their ingredients, and thoroughly forgive ourselves or those who have contributed to their being. During this journey of self-discovery, it will almost certainly become clear how and why the angry thought forms turned into physical or mental disease. It will become equally clear that they are an integral part of the person, not a scourge arbitrarily imposed from outside. This realization is often the turning point in a patient's illness. Because that which has been created by someone's thinking can equally be dissolved by it, the patient is freed from despair and from a feeling of helplessness. He can move on to the next stage of self-healing.

To realize that the past is malleable is to be released from its power. It is not what happens to us that is important but what one does with it once it has happened. We cannot change the actual events of the past, but by changing our thoughts about them, we can prevent them from destroying us through disease. They can instead be transformed into opportunities for learning. If our disease is the logical result of the thinking and emotions evoked by past events, then these thought-patterns and emotional patterns *must* be radically changed. Until this change is made, the channelling of healing to self can not take place, because it will be constantly blocked by the old angers and resentments.

The element of violence inherent in all severe loss inevitably causes shock. This applies to anything which was held very dear or which was vital to the patient's self-image, whether it was loss of a person, a house, money or status. Such a shock is one of the commonest causes of severe illness, although it is not always recognized as such because it is often delayed. Again an honest assessment of the situation is vital if the patient is to prevent himself from becoming ill. Starting to peel away the alien, destructive elements from his loss is a difficult and often painful task. But if he is willing and able to do this, he may well gain new

115

wisdom which would not have come to him through more gentle events. He may even eventually reach a point where he can be thankful to his suffering for the enlightenment it has brought him.

The cure of cancer through visualization is clearly an extreme example of self-healing, but it illustrates our basic tenet that we have far more control over our bodies than we have been led to believe by most modern doctors. They have done us a great disservice by taking on to themselves such complete responsibility for our health that a patient in the Western world hardly participates in his own healing. He opens his mouth to receive his prescribed drugs; if he is told that he needs an operation, he submits to it. Usually he receives only the scantiest explanation of his condition and its possible consequences or dangers, nor is he told what he himself can do to speed his own healing. This situation must change. Our most potent ally in the search for wholeness and health, the patient himself, is being wasted.

If, on the contrary, the patient's whole Being and strength is mustered to help his own recovery, astounding results can be achieved, as in the case of a 68 year old woman who was admitted to hospital with severe abdominal pain. After examination and a biopsy, she was diagnosed as having stomach cancer. Her reaction to this was categoric: she would *not* submit to an operation; she would deal with the situation herself. Through diet and meditation she embarked, entirely alone, on a path of self-healing. When she was killed in a car accident five years later, her autopsy revealed no signs of cancer.

It was only after her death that it became apparent to her three children, who all lived in different countries abroad, how profound had been the voyage of self-discovery through which their mother had regained her health. From having been constantly at war with herself, anxious and indecisive, she had become a leader. Instead of being fearful and tentative in her relationships with her children, she had become very positive with both them and her grandchildren. The change in her had been so subtle and slow that it was only through piecing together the evidence

116

that they understood the extraordinary transformation which she had realized in herself.

What the above patient was able to achieve through absorbing into herself that which had caused her illness, another patient accomplished with the help of someone who had been very close to her and had died fifteen years earlier. This middle-aged woman, very unhappily married, had for many years been an unrecognized alcoholic. When she at last admitted to her doctor that the situation had become critical, she found that because she was unwilling to resign all responsibility for her own condition and go into a Home for addicts where drink would be forcibly withheld from her, she would somehow have to heal herself. It was at this point, faced with an apparently enormously difficult task, that she was given the help which cured her physically and allowed her to move into an entirely new phase of understanding and growth. She described this help as the hand of her daughter clasping hers in complete love and firmness. She even heard the child's voice promise a successful outcome to the struggle. This collaboration succeeded immediately and decisively because of her initial recognition that she had reached a crisis point in her life. By allowing herself to accept help, she had healed herself of the need for slow self-destruction. Although the deep-rooted problems of her marriage and of her own fears were not yet resolved, at least she could now face them with open eyes.

Meditation

If self-healing depends basically on self-knowledge, meditation becomes one of our most important allies. To search for our 'still centre' is hard work but it is an endlessly rewarding and creative occupation, from there we can begin to receive the help and teaching which are so freely offered to us once we learn to listen. This search requires devotion and patience but as our intuition and awareness grow, we begin to realize our vast potential for repairing the hurts done to us by ourselves and others. And what

117

began as a repair job often turns into creativity at whatever level we are capable of expressing ourselves. Once past the initial stage of pain that most people have to endure when first confronting their uncensored selves, this journey of self-discovery and regeneration gradually produces a very positive joy. The loneliness and sense of isolation which is at the root of so much modern disease can never again overcome us, for we have become part of the whole world, past, present and future.

In the learning and practice of meditation, two recently-invented machines have proved most helpful. Max Cade and Geoffrey Blundell have developed a simple biofeedback machine which straps on to your hand and monitors your state of relaxation. The term biofeedback simply means that the machine is feeding back information about a process being undergone by your body. The machine is not *teaching* you meditation. But by recording your progress, it makes you very accurately conscious of how the meditative state should feel. This recognition, based on visible evidence, helps you learn meditation more quickly than by traditional methods.

The Mind Mirror, also invented by Cade and Blundell, is more complex. With electric pads attached to your head, it records your brain waves in a series of tiny light bulbs which form different patterns corresponding to different states of mind: the active everyday state, the state of meditation, and the state of healing. Again the machine is a most helpful aid to learning.

One of the greatest difficulties for most Westerners learning to meditate is the fact that it has been taught almost exclusively by people trained in the Eastern traditions of religion and philosophy. For them stillness and passivity are familiar concepts, and their teaching is based on the assumption that we should – and can – still our everyday minds in order to meditate. By the use of a Mantra (a monotonously repeated sound), they seek to create a vacuum into which teaching can pour from higher sources.

But there are two problems here. First of all there is danger in creating a vacuum in the psyche of someone who is without any training in spiritual disciplines and who is not under the close supervision of a teacher. Where there is a vacuum, undesirable ideas can enter as readily as can desirable teaching. Secondly the Western mind is not geared to this inactive approach. We have been brought up to *do* things, to *build*, to use our time *achieving* something. The whole exercise then seems to us negative, producing a sense of guilt and restless unease. Many people then abandon meditation, saying either that it makes no sense, or that it is only suitable for those who are leading a contemplative life. This is very sad, because creative meditation can be the greatest help and joy to everyone. It brings intensification of concentration and an easing of stress which makes anyone more effective whatever his occupation.

Is there then an approach to Meditation better suited to twentieth century Western man? The Maharishi has developed, with great success, Transcendental Meditation, or T.M., which has brought relaxation and physical well-being to many thousands in both Europe and America. But for those who find his teaching a little slick and superficial, what else is there on offer?

The European equivalent of meditation has been taught by the Church ever since the advent of Christianity. The practice of contemplation has sought, through disciplines which overcome the ego, to unite man with God. But these disciplines are, in a different way, as unsuitable as the traditions of Eastern Gurus, both of which assume that the search for God or Otherness is the central concern of a person's life. As this is the case for only a small minority, we must look for yet another Way.

For the exteriorized, active Westerner, the idea of creating through visualization a place in which to meditate is usually easier than emptying or stilling the mind. This special place in his imagination, whether it is a garden, a favourite spot by the sea, or a meadow in the mountains, must be completely vivid to all his senses. It must also be reached on a symbolic level by a bridge or gate which links him to his inner silence and cuts him off from the rest of the world, so that by going there he is separated from his everyday life and thoughts and thus reaches at least part of that detachment which the Eastern teaching achieves by more abstract methods. This bridge or gate symbolizes his entrance and exit into a different state of consciousness. It also helps preserve within the meditation place the stillness which is built up there each day, so that it remains undisturbed and readily available.

As an example of this visualization technique, let us imagine a garden. The wall surrounding it is of white-washed bricks; its gate is made of wrought iron. It is summertime, very early in the morning. You are alone. You shut the garden gate quietly behind you; the grey slate of the path feels cool and rough under your bare feet. You walk slowly along the path, observing in detail the colours and shapes of all the different flowers. There is a magnolia tree in the centre of the garden and a small weeping willow by the edge of a pond. The water is still, reflecting the clouds between the water lilies which have not yet opened. The birds are hardly awake and the sounds they make are soft and peaceful. You sit down on a stone bench, drawing into yourself the harmony of the garden and the animals who have slept there. You are so quiet that a rabbit passes close to your bench and a squirrel darts up the tree behind you. Sitting there with your back straight, your feet firm on the ground and your hands lying palm upwards in your lap, you shut your eyes. You breathe long, deep breaths that still you yet further. If bothersome, practical thoughts intrude on you, push them gently aside, asking them to wait a little while. Don't fight them or be annoyed at yourself for having allowed them in; that will only give them strength. Stay in your silence for as long as you are comfortable, then return gradually into the sunshine. Open your eyes slowly; move your hands and feet, give thanks for the peace you have found. Then walk quietly back along the path. Be sure to close the gate behind you.

When you first start this exercise, you will probably achieve only a sense of peace and relaxation, but gradually your meditations will become deeper and more rewarding, helping to expand and enrich your life, giving it a unity and joyfulness which will be of great help to you and everyone you meet.

A few more brief points: whatever method of meditation you use, it is important to establish a routine. Ideally you should be in the same place at the same time every day, preferably in the early morning when your mind is still free from daily chores. This will give a ritualistic quality to the exercise which is very helpful. If you travel a lot, try at least to set aside your special time of day, and use some symbol, such as the lighting of a candle, to shift you quickly into the meditative state. Protect yourself from outside disturbances such as the telephone, the doorbell, or noisy children; sit in semi-darkness so that your eyes are not strained against the light. A straight-backed, armless chair is the best; your feet should be firmly on the floor, preferably without shoes. Your clothes should be comfortable so that you are not aware of a tight belt, constricting collar, etc.

Self-Knowledge

Self-healing, whether physical or psychological, requires a great deal of courage. At times this process cannot be started alone; a catalyst is needed to help take you into a new period of growth. The person who acts as the catalyst need not be a professional therapist, it can be a friend or even a stranger. He may start the process in a dozen different ways: by lending you a book, for instance, or listening to you with total attention. It may take five minutes or be a dialogue continued over several weeks. But in some way, by a look or a word, or even a silence, he will have been the instrument for the first stage of your release. Crucial to you for a short time, when you were too unwell or too dispersed to act on your own, he will then leave you to face your disease or your problem on your own. But by then you will be strengthened enough to do so.

Once convinced that self-knowledge, however painful, is preferable to the unknown and the unresolved, you can make use of your new awareness to begin interpreting the signals from your body which you have until now disregarded. Your self-healing will probably start from a physical level: time and love spent on learning methods of relaxation or improving your diet and sleeping habits may well be so rewarding that you begin to see yourself as a whole over whom you have far more control than you ever imagined. The lack of good health which you have endured for so long that you almost took it for granted will suddenly seem unnecessary and ridiculous, and your self-healing will start, through self-knowledge, to spread its effects to some psychological wound. This may be something which has for so long affected all your relationships that you no longer recognized the emptiness or the distortions which it had been causing. But by dealing with it, your work will be able to progress to a yet deeper level: a spiritual one. From there you could well reach the certainty that because man is essentially a spiritual being, true self-healing – that which can make you transcend yourself – will come to you when all doubts and unrest between yourself and God are repaired.

Because many people, especially those who have been brought up in England, were taught that it is wrong to burden others with their troubles, a stubborn independance makes them try to solve their own problems; they find it very difficult to accept help from anyone else. But this is not sensible. In a way it is even selfish, because it is denying someone else the joy of giving. To stand in isolation, refusing help, is to deny the fact of our common humanity. If we are all one, then the sadness and chaos of any individual affects everyone else, and we should accept any help that can make us whole and happy.

As long as we do not let friends become props, in the same way that we should not become dependant on drugs and doctors, we should welcome the opportunity to have our self-healing speeded and deepened by others when the time is right. The only thing we must never do is to let anyone hurry us. Each of us, in each phase of our life, has a certain tempo at which we are able to progress. If an apparently 'instant' healing occurs, it is in reality usually the final stage in a series of minor healings brought about by our own new self-knowledge and enlightenment. It is the rounding-off of a certain cycle of development. But in the same way that we may have needed someone else to help us start on this cycle, we may have needed someone to help us complete it, and we should welcome that help.

Learning to Become a Healer

Healing oneself and giving healing to others are closely interrelated, and it seems that it is quite often when a new stage of the former occurs in someone that he finds in himself the ability to be a healer. It is as though by creating a good relationship within himself he is able to link up with someone else. By ridding himself of some aspect of selfishness, he has freed a channel that can be used for focusing the Life Force on to a patient. It is a continuing process whereby the more he can learn and improve, the better healer he will become, and the more healing he gives, the more he will receive. Gradually his whole life will be taken over by this process.

If we can envisage being a healer as part of the cycle of self-healing, let us consider what should be done by the increasing number of people who are finding in themselves the ability to heal. If someone is not yet certain whether he is really meant to be developing his healing potential, he should start by becoming acutely attentive both to outward events and to his own inner dialogue. He will then almost certainly receive some sort of sign. There are many possible ways by which the message could reach him, but two things are certain: firstly, if his gift is only imagined this will soon be made clear to him; and secondly, however small or great it is, it must eventually be developed to its utmost.

The best way of starting to learn is to find a practising healer who will take you on as apprentice. This will give you confidence in the quickest and safest way possible. It

123

will also prevent you from getting out of your depth on your own, and teach you the possible pitfalls. You should also go to some reputable course to learn the basics about energy interchanges and how to discipline and direct them. There are also vital lessons to learn about loss of energy, which can be such a severe danger to a healer. It is not enough to lay your hands on a patient and direct energy to him, you must also learn to detach yourself from the patient once the healing is finished, otherwise your electromagnetic field, or aura, will remain confounded with that of the patient, and your energy will be sapped.

Another thing that a healer must learn from the start is that it is *not* he who is giving the healing. He is only a channel through which God or the Life Force is flowing. Many beginners feel that they are committing the sin of pride in imagining that they could heal someone, and because of this fear they dismiss the possibility of becoming a healer instead of learning to fulfil their potential. But once they realize that they are only a channel, pride no longer plays any part. They can only feel awe and wonder at being used in such a way, and hope that they will slowly evolve to the stage where they can help their patients to reach that inner trust which ultimately disposes of fear, even the fear of death.

7 Healing Today

Many patients who are new to healing find it disturbing that nothing visible or tangible is being done to them. An unknown energy is said to have been transmitted to them through the healer's hands, but has it really affected them? Are they only imagining results? Is it really true that thoughts and attitudes can have such potent effects on their bodies? It may well take some time before a patient feels comfortable, in differing degrees and for different reasons, with the basic concepts of healing.

In the meantime, any of the other forms of complementary medicine, the ones that include mechanical aids such as radionics, acupuncture, colour healing etc., are more easily acceptable. There he can see that something, however unfamiliar, is being done, and so the dials of the radionics machine, the needles of the acupuncturist, or the oils of the aromatherapist serve as a form of communication between healer and patient. As detailed accounts of these other therapies are beyond the scope of this book, I will discuss them only in their relationship with hand healing.

Basically, all the other therapies are compatible with, and can be enhanced by, hand healing. It could even be argued that as they are using physical means to achieve the same result as hand healing, that is to say the redistribution and

125

balancing of the body's energies, a combination of hand healing and another therapy can be the most beneficial, both physically and psychologically, to a patient who is still uncertain about the various therapies, or who is so seriously ill that he needs every available support.

Which of the therapies he chooses is, in a sense, not of primary importance. They are all promoting healing by stimulating the body's capacity for self-healing and by re-establishing its harmony. But the quality of the therapist is a vital consideration. At the time of writing, while practitioners – especially in the country – are few in number, a therapy might well be selected because of the abilities of its local exponent.

If, however, there is a choice between equally capable practitioners of several different therapies, the next most important consideration is the patient himself. Depending on whether he is fundamentally scientific, artistic, or mystical, what education he has received, what religious views he holds, and in which group he would feel most at ease, he will progress better in one therapy than another, perhaps not even realizing for a long time why his particular choice was made.

The question of the disease concerned is the final consideration. All the therapies would claim to benefit a wide spectrum of illnesses; logically there is no reason why any illness should be excluded from any therapy as all forms of healing aim to restore to its original pattern that which has become distorted. Chiropratic, for instance, being primarily concerned with the spine, would seem the obvious choice for someone who had dislocated a vertebra; yet any of the other complementary therapists would also hope to ameliorate such a condition. Equally, the chiropractor would tell you that his treatment could improve any other part of the body as much as the spine through which he works directly.

The most important elements of all, then, are the patient's attitude of mind, the healer's ability, and the relationship between healer and patient. The amount of help someone receives will depend upon his readiness to accept it and the therapist's power to transmit it. As these grow with mutual trust, so will the healing reach a deeper and deeper level of the patient's being, affecting not only his body but his psyche and soul. The results are limited only by the growth potential of the patient and healer.

In the following, touching case of a young woman who was not expected to live more than a few weeks after her third operation for cancer, we can see the drastic effect that real self-knowledge and a change of heart can have, especially if they are reinforced by an understanding healer. In a state of extreme exhaustion and sickness from her chemo-therapy and cobalt treatment, compelled to face her imminent death, she began talking to the healer from a depth of herself which she had never before even considered. Gradually, as she told him about the self-centred promiscuous life she had led as a student, she understood that by totally disregarding her body and never admitting to her spiritual existence, she had brought into herself this potentially lethal illness. As she came to recognize how little she had once valued life and how much she now wanted to live, she saw that, even at this late stage, understanding of her behaviour and self-forgiveness could halt the destructive process. It was possibly her enormous courage in attempting to reverse a ten-year process in a few weeks which saved her. She has done much irreversible damage to her body and will never be a physically fit person again, but she has survived, and has a sense of unity and rhythm within herself which makes her a hundred times stronger, more purposeful, and happier than she was before her illness.

In this story of a very remarkable girl, the healer played an almost passive role. He was a sounding board for what she herself had already begun to uncover. But she needed that sounding board. She also needed his belief in her to evoke the courage and conviction which were already very near the surface of her being. Because of his reassurance that she was not attempting the impossible, she was able to summon up all her forces of self-healing and at the same time make herself receptive to his healing powers. That he could express, as an acceptable concept, the possibility that she would be given a second chance was also of prime importance to her intellect, allowing it to work with her instead of undermining by its disbelief her new and fragile confidence.

In the following case the healer had a more active role to play because his patient had not yet reached such a high degree of awareness. He was a man typical of many cases where *rigidity* is one of a person's predominant characteristics. The type of rigidity with which we are here concerned can manifest in many different ways: it can produce extremely set religious beliefs; it can be displayed as discipline and tidiness carried to extremes; or it can express itself in an unbending attitude towards people, according them very little forgiveness for the slightest transgression. But whatever outward form the rigidity takes, it stems from an inability to accept the tiniest deviation from the world pattern the individual has decreed. Such a psychological state, which often includes uncompromising bitterness and resentment, must – like all other states of mind – sooner or later affect the physical body. And, as always, the quality of the mind is reflected in the quality of the disease. A harsh outlook will produce some form of physical hardness and this is often arthritis, where the joints become unwilling and eventually unable to bend.

The patient in question was a man of fifty who had consulted the healer as a last resort and at the instigation of his wife. He had very little self-understanding, and the possibility of his attaining any was blocked by his resentment against his illness. The healer's difficulty here was how to capture his patient's interest quickly enough to prevent him from abandoning the treatment. The inflexibility of the man's attitude made it difficult for the healing to effect him, but at least his acute pain was quickly eased, and from there the first steps could be taken. Tentative confidence was established. Their talk deepened.

The problem, it appeared eventually, stemmed from an acutely unhappy father/son relationship. Never as a boy or a young man had he been allowed to be himself; always he

128

had been the projection of a very powerful and self-willed father who had cast him in the role of business man, (successor in the family firm), without any regard for his inclinations or talents. Instead of going to university and studying music, he began at the age of eighteen to learn the whisky trade. His bitter resentment against his father, combined with the claustrophobia of being trapped in a way of life which was alien to him and which he had been quite unable to transcend, had been too much for him. Because he could not bend anything surrounding him, he forbade the slightest bending in anyone else, and his family was suffering as much as he from the cause and result of his bitterness.

His therapy took a very long time. For there to be an unbending from within, a real desire to change in order to be healed, he had to recognize his own part in the forming of his disease, but it was an in-built element of his personality not to be able to see his own faults or to assess himself in a new light; he *could* not imagine himself as an initiator rather than a victim. But eventually, much helped by his wife who also visited the healer, his carapace began to crack. The healing was absorbed with increasing rapidity. Eventually there was very little stiffness left in his joints. From there it was not too difficult to revise his whole way of life: when business no longer dominated him, and his music took on increasing importance, he was almost able to enjoy his work, and he was certainly much better at it.

Where a very strong psychic link exists between two people, an interesting phenomenon can take place: a person can be cured via someone else. This can happen either intentionally or unintentionally.

As an example of treatment being given with intent through a third party, I would like to cite the case of a woman who had suffered for several years with a very painful, congenital back ailment. When she and her husband moved two hundred miles away from her practitioner, in whom she had great confidence, she refused to consult anyone else. Then one day she was confined to bed in such pain that her husband decided to go and consult their former doctor. Between them they devised an experiment. While they both held a picture of the patient firmly in mind and concentrated together on the maladjustment in her spine which was causing the pain, the husband's back was manipulated. His wife became free of pain at that moment. She could not have imagined it, as she knew nothing of what they were doing. From then on, her husband was able to receive healing on her behalf whenever necessary. The fact that the generalized ache in his own spine cleared when he was transmitting healing to his wife was an added bonus for him!

In another instance the healing sent to a critically ill woman was unwittingly transmitted to her husband, who had suffered for many years from acute rheumatism, giving him great pain and a very bad temper. After this particular healing, she was herself no better and awoke the next morning in despair from a restless and pain-ridden night. Her husband, on the contrary, was not only physically improved, he had also experienced a profound change of personality. From being the basic cause of his wife's unhappiness and illness, he became during her final weeks a most loving help. It seemed as though the conscious intent of the healer to bring the wife physical relief had been disregarded in favour of a more far-reaching healing of the couple through the husband.

Basically, though, the factor of prime importance is the patient's participation in the healing. If he or she refuses to understand what has caused the illness and cannot help to transmute these basic causes into something creative, then the help available from the healer is extremely limited. It may be able temporarily to alleviate some physical symptoms, but it cannot really achieve anything deeper. This fact was vividly illustrated in the case of a man in his forties who had suffered a classic stress heart attack. As a result of the damage to his heart recorded on the hospital's electro-cardiogram, his insurance premium was heavily increased. Following this incident, the patient continued to complain of pain in the thoracic area of his spine, and of the same breathlessness he had known before the attack. He was obviously very anxious about the possibility of a further one. Healing and the manipulation of his spine were only able to allay his symptoms temporarily. Gradually however his basic problem emerged: a childhood spent with a series of foster parents. As the anxiety and uncertainty of those years surfaced and were dealt with, so his health improved until finally his electrocardiogram registered a healthily functioning heart – and his insurance premium returned to its normal status.

The question of participation also enters into a patient's dying. In this sense dying should be considered as an integral part of healing. Everyone must one day die, and for a patient to do so should not automatically be considered a failure of healing. To die in full consciousness and peace can be the ultimate healing of all that has been ragged and unresolved in the rest of a lifetime. There are of course occasions such as instantaneous accidental deaths when this is not possible, but here presumably other processes are involved, and the resolution of the past must be differently achieved. But in a death from illness, where the patient has time to form a relationship between himself and death, the question of participation is of prime importance.

Whether or not someone should be told when he is mortally ill is the first dilemma to resolve. If death is to be considered as something active in which we have every right, and indeed every duty, to participate, then anyone who can possibly benefit from knowing of his own impending death should presumably know. This is, of course, a very personal question which can only be answered by a close relation or friend, or by a doctor well acquainted with the patient. Alternatively people should perhaps be encouraged, while still in good health, to express their wishes on this subject, and these wishes should then be respected whatever the feelings and inclinations of those who have to implement them.

The following case illustrates the potential inherent in the process of 'conscious' dying. A woman asked her young daughter to promise not to keep her in ignorance but

131

to tell her if she – the mother – ever contracted a fatal illness. The daughter made this promise, as it seemed right for someone like her mother who had conducted an orderly life and would presumably want to die in the same way. The mother was also a person of great courage, so that even though she had very little religious or spiritual life she would, her daughter felt, find the fortitude to face the situation when it arose. Ten years passed and then the academic question became a practical one: the mother had cancer. The family wanted to hide this fact from her. They said she must be allowed to end her life happily. To tell her of her illness would be both cruel and unconstructive. The daughter stood firm. She had, she said, made a promise and she respected her mother enough to think that she knew what she really wanted. Incurring the fury of everyone around her, she kept her promise.

There were several loose ends in the mother's life: relationships within and outside the family, and above all relationships with her childhood and her own mother. As the weeks progressed and she gradually sorted these out, the peace grew within her, and the first links with her spiritual self were formed. She died quietly, having done as much as she could, glad to have been given those healing months, which could not have been nearly as fruitful had she been unaware of her imminent death.

Let us now consider how some of the therapies available to us relate to hand healing and to orthodox medicine.

Chiropracty and Osteopathy

These two therapies probably provide the most acceptable bridge between orthodoxy and healing. Because their practitioners have a scientific training, based on a recognizable anatomical plan, they do not generate the same sense of mystification as some of the other therapies. Even though osteopaths and chiropractors are not officially accepted by the medical profession, many doctors, for years, have been unofficially referring patients to them for conditions involving the spinal column, for accidents, or

132

for congenital defects relating to the bones. To any patient with a scientific background, the atmosphere and functioning of an osteopath's or chiropractor's consulting room – which often includes such recognizable aids as an X-ray machine – could seem very reassuring, and he would respond easily to a healer working in conjunction with these professions.

Referrals to these therapists are mainly for recurring back conditions not serious enough to require surgery or for pain, mainly in the neck and shoulder area, caused by tension. But there are many other conditions where manipulation can be most helpful. Accidents frequently produce lesions and stiffness which are perfect sites for arthritis and rheumatism; keeping the patient supple can often forestall these conditions. Bad posture is another condition helped by manipulation, especially if the patient is young and his patterns can be changed to prevent discomfort from becoming chronic pain. A healer could enhance the effect of any of these treatments. Working on the fundamental causes of the stress or the bad posture (which is so often the outward expression of shyness or insecurity), he would build up the patient's general health and confidence, thereby making permanent the good done by the osteopath.

In the case of accidents, a healer's help could be equally valuable. Shock remains in our bodies far longer and with far more deleterious effect than is generally realized. By releasing the shock, he could spare his patient a wide range of possible ill effects, both physical and psychological.

Acupuncture

In the past ten years, acupuncture has developed from a 'way out' therapy to an almost respectable Harley Street activity. But although new to us, acupuncture is one of the oldest traditions of medicine. In China and many far Eastern countries it has been for thousands of years the orthodox therapy – used, in conjunction with herbal medicine, for all eventualities including anaesthesia in

133

surgery. It is based on the principle that two forms of energy, the Yin and Yang, should ideally flow freely and in balance throughout our body. If blockages occur in this flow, pain and disease follow. The body has both major and minor acupuncture points, and it is into these that the acupuncturists' needles are placed to release the blockages. Most doctors, unfamiliar with this concept of an energy flow which does not exist in Western medicine, are contemptuous or afraid of acupuncture; but an increasing number are beginning to admit that its results, whatever its theory, are often satisfactory. Here however *particular* care should be given to selecting a therapist. Because of the sudden extensive growth of acupuncture, many inadequately-trained people are practising it.

As in chiropracty or osteopathy, patients with scientific leanings feel more at home with acupuncture than with certain other therapies. Even though its charting of the human body is unfamiliar to Westerners, it does use diagrams. Here again a particularly fruitful partnership could exist between a hand-healer and another branch of complementary medicine, the healer reinforcing the effect of the acupuncturist's needles and 'moxsa' which, according to certain clairvoyants, have the same effect on the body as a healer's energy.

Homoeopathy

Homoeopathy, which has been practised in Europe for the past 160 years, is another therapy which has at least one familiar link with orthodox medicine: it treats its patients with pills. The fact that the preparation and composition of these pills is entirely different from that of allopathic medicine is somehow less alarming to many people than the theories behind certain complementary therapies. Many hand-healers work with a homoeopath and whatever remedies he gives the patient, their potency can be affirmed by the healer. Here is another alliance which should be especially productive as the homoeopath and the healer both work on the same basic principle: the

134

whole patient must be treated rather than a specific disease.

The number of people attracted to this form of medicine is growing rapidly. Not only are they increasingly frightened by the power of modern drugs and their sometimes unknown potential for harm, there are also many people who fear the dependance on medicines wilfully encouraged by the drug companies and tacitly condoned by our over-worked general practitioners. There are also few people now unaware that new forms of disease are being constantly created by the side-effects of drugs. The extent of this phenomenon is perhaps less widely realized: many patients in both American and European hospitals are suffering from drug-induced diseases. As this state of affairs becomes increasingly publicized, more people will certainly be drawn towards gentler and safer forms of medication.

Radionics

Radionics is a system of healing based on the theory that each organ of the body has a distinct vibrational rate and that when that rate is disturbed, the organ manifests disease. The radionics machine, by emitting vibrations of the correct rate to the diseased organ, restores its balance and health. This process can take place in the presence or absence of the patient as the radionics emission, like a healer's energy, are not affected by space. Although this whole theory is untenable to most scientists, who do not admit the existence of these vibrationary rates, radionics does at least derive from a rational premise and functions with visible instruments, so that it too can be a reassuring therapy for a new patient.

Many hand-healers work as a team with a radionics practitioner not only for treating a patient but also for diagnosing his condition. Radionics diagnosis is done with a 'pendulum' or small dowsing instrument which gives the practitioner negative or affirmative responses. First of all an anatomical chart is used to locate the site of the disease, then the exact trouble is pinpointed by consulting a detailed list of possible diseases. This same technique can be used to discover the causes of allergies. Working from a list of possible allergenic substances, the movement of the pendulum indicates which of them is harmful to the patient. This is a very speedy process compared to the more conventional method of testing the substance by placing samples on the patient's skin or under his tongue. (The latter method can also be extremely unpleasant for anyone dramatically allergic to something, who may manifest symptoms ranging from intense itching to uncontrollable fits.)

Because it is a therapy which works at a distance (although most practitioners like to see a patient at least once before starting treatment), radionics plus absent healing are an ideal combination for patients who travel a lot or who live far from any therapist. A strong radionics practitioner teamed up with a good absent healer can generate a very formidable power. But here again it is important to remember that the therapy is only as good as its practitioner: the radionics 'black box' can almost be considered as a magnifying instrument for the healing emitted by its operator. If he has no healing power, the machine alone is virtually powerless.

Chromotherapy

This therapy, also known as colour healing, is one which will appeal to anyone of artistic temperament. It confirms through science what has always been known intuitively by those who are sensitive to colour: each different shade and tone has its own healing property. Like radionics, this system of healing is based on the principle of vibrations. Each colour radiates energy at a different vibratory rate, starting at the lower end of the scale with dense red and ending up with the most refined and swiftly-vibrating purple. Here again it is essentially the person rather than the disease which must be treated because the deepest, most vital elements of a person's temperament will always need certain colours, whatever others he or she is

136

temporarily lacking through disease. For instance, broadly speaking, a lethargic person is nearly always in need of red, whereas a choleric temperament needs to be soothed with green or blue before any more detailed treatment can be given to him. A patient will also react to a colour with greater or lesser intensity depending on the essential colours of his own temperament.

The means whereby colour is directed to a patient vary from coloured lamps to pure thought. When thought is used, the practitioner is acting almost like a hand healer, except that he is concentrating on a specific section of the spectrum rather than on Light, which is the sum total of all colours. Some radionics practitioners combine colour therapy with their emissions, each set of vibrations intensifying the efficacy of the other.

Different diseases require different colours for their treatment. Their classification, however, is neither as stringently defined nor as universally employed as are the vibratory rates used in radionics. Because colours are sub-divided into such a multiplicity of tones and shades, and are seen in such a personal way, colour therapy is extremely difficult to regimentalize and to teach. Its success is, perhaps more than for any other existing treatment, dependant on the ability of the individual therapist.

Another reason why colour therapy is such a personal process is that growing sensitivity enables the therapist to differentiate between increasingly subtle shades. As this knowledge can only be communicated in the most general terms, each colour healer tends to evolve his own system according to his own intuition and experience. As long as this fact is accepted and he is not condemned for failing to conform to someone else's theories and classifications, all is well. But this does mean that a patient must discover for himself someone with whom he is in tune rather than relying on certificates of proficiency from a school. We are told that in the New Age new and subtler colours will become visible to the human eye. Colour therapy in the coming years should then grow in importance as its range of effectiveness expands.

137

In certain healing disciplines such as the White Eagle Lodge, colour is used for protective work as well as for the alleviation of specific diseases. The deep, velvet blue associated with the Virgin Mary's robes, and a beautiful gold, are the colours most frequently used to protect someone who is in danger of physical, psychic or psychological attack.

Massage

There are several forms of massage, both new and old, which are growing in popularity. Their practitioners are usually people with naturally healing hands who have extended their capacity to heal through the use of either Shiatsu (a traditional Japanese massage), acupressure (a massage which uses the same meridians as acupuncture), aromatherapy (based on an ancient method of massage which makes use of essential oils to help re-balance the body), or a number of others. As well as the specific good done by these healing massages, they are invaluable in helping people to become more aware of their bodies and the various strains to which they are being subjected. As we gradually realize that there is a happy medium between self-indulgence and self-denial, these various forms of massage will help us establish more friendly relationships with our bodies.

Any form of massage could be used beneficially in conjunction with hand healing. Again, the massage would afford a new patient tangible proof that help was being given to him, and this would make it easier for him to receive the unseen energies of hand healing. The healer could also promote and continue the work instigated by the massage, which stirs stagnant parts of the body into activity. As muscles and joints are revivified by a new flow of energy, and the circulation and skin are stimulated, acids and toxins which have accumulated through wrong diet, fatigue, stress, disease etc. are released into the body. By helping to disperse these, the healer will prevent headaches or temporary exhaustion, because a deep

138

massage has much the same effect as a fast: by renewing or re-orientating the body, it can make the patient feel weak and uncomfortable before he derives benefit from it.

Reflexology

Reflexology is another interesting therapy. Using very detailed charts, which map out the correspondence between certain points on the feet and various parts of the body, the reflexologist massages the foot with his thumbs. Disease can be diagnosed as a thickening or heaviness at these specific points; the diagnosis will be quickly confirmed by the patient as a stabbing pain. The treatment used by the reflexologist is curiously similar to his diagnostic methods: he continues to massage with his thumbs in a deep twisting motion which gradually releases the blockage of energy which has been causing pain or malfunction.

Although we have not been able to deal with the full range of complementary therapies available, we hope to have established the extent to which they can help each other and also enhance the efficacy of orthodox medicine.

The world is changing, perhaps more radically than we have yet realized. And the most profound change of all will be in man himself. As we evolve, we will realize that we *must* take responsibility for our own bodies, psyches and souls. We can no longer be treated as children from whom the all-knowing adult demands unquestioning obedience. Healers will help us to discover for ourselves what is best for us. And as this new attitude spreads, we will find that it is not only individuals who are being healed, but the planet itself. In the same way that people will realize that they can no longer tolerate strong drugs, they will understand that the earth cannot tolerate the violence of the fertilizers and insecticides we have been imposing upon it. As we start treating our bodies kindly we will stop upsetting our planet's delicate balance. Once we have seen ourselves as whole and as part of the earth, we will welcome our interdependence with it, and healing on a major scale will begin to take place. Ecology will no longer be seen as eccentric, but as an urgent necessity. Then we will be able to start growing to our full potential, whose significance and possibilities we have hardly begun to comprehend. Intimately linked both to the earth and to the Life Force, it will be as infinite as that Life Force itself.

Bibliography and Suggested Further Reading

ANDERTON, William *Inner Alchemy* (Soluna 1981)

ASSAGIOLI, Roberto *Psychosynthesis* (Turnstone Press, London, 1975)

AUROBINDO, Sri *The Future Evolution of Man* (Theosophical Publishing House Quest, London, 1974)

BACH, Richard *Jonathan Livingstone Seagull* (Turnstone Press, London, 1974)

BAILEY, Alice *Esoteric Healing* (Lucis Press, London, 1967)

CAPRA, Fritjof *The Tao of Physics* (Wildwood House, London, 1975)
Turning Point (Wildwood House, London, 1982)

FORTUNE, Dion *The Esoteric Philosophy of Love and Marriage* (Aquarian Press, London, 1974)

GREAVES, Helen *Testimony of Light* (Neville Spearman, Sudbury, 1969)

GREENE, Liz *Relating* (Coventure, London, 1977)

GUIRDHAM, Arthur *We are One Another* (Neville Spearman, Sudbury, 1974)

INGLIS, Brian *Natural Medicine* (Fontana, London, 1980)

JOHNSTON, William *Silent Music* (Fontana, London, 1974)
The Inner Eye of Love (Collins, London, 1978)

Jung, Carl Gustav *Memories, Dreams and Reflections* (Fontana, London, 1967)

Kubler-Ross, Dr. Elizabeth *On Death and Dying* (Tavistock, London, 1973)

Lehmann, Rosamund and Tudor Pole, Welsley *My dear Alexias* (Neville Spearman, Sudbury, 1979)

Le Shan, Lawrence *Clairvoyant Reality* (Turnstone Press, London, 1980)
How To Meditate, A guide To Self-Discovery (Turnstone Press, London, 1983)

Levi, A. *The Aquarian Gospel of Jesus the Christ* (Fowler, Romford, 1964)

Mackarness, Dr. Richard *Not All in the Mind* (Pan, London, 1976)

Moody *Life after Life* (Bantam, London, 1976)

Nicoll, Maurice *The New Man* (Watkins, London, 1981)

Rendel, Peter *Introduction To The Chakras* (Aquarian Press, London, 1979)

Rushforth, Winifred *Something is Happening* (Turnstone, London, 1981)

Saint Exupery, A. *The Little Prince* (Heinemann, London, 1945)

Sandys, Cynthia and Lehmann, Rosamund *The Awakening Letters* (Neville Spearman, Sudbury, 1978)

Schumacher, E. *Small is Beautiful* (Blond and Briggs, London, 1973)

Schwaller de Lubicz Isha *The Opening of the Way* (Inner Traditions 1981)

Shattock, Admiral, E. H. *A Manual of Self Healing* (Turnstone Press, London, 1982)

Singer, June *Androgyny* (Routledge & Kegan Paul, London, 1977)

Steiner, Rudolf *Knowledge of The Higher Worlds* (Rudolf Steiner Press, 1969)

Szekely, Edmond Bordeaux *The Teaching of the Essenes* (C. W. Daniel, Saffron Walden, 1978)

Trevelyan, Sir George *Operation Redemption* (Turnstone Press, London, 1981)

142

TUDOR POLE, Welsley *Writing on the Ground* (Neville Spearman, Sudbury, 1968)

VAN DER POST, Laurens *Jung and the Story of Our Time* (Hogarth Press, London, 1976)
The Seed and The Sower (Hogarth Press, London, 1963)

WATSON, Lyall *The Romeo Error* (Hodder & Stoughton, Sevenoaks, 1976)

WILSON, Colin *The War Against Sleep* (Aquarian Press, London, 1980)

WILSON, Annie and BEK, Lilla *What Colour Are You?* (Turnstone Press, London, 1981)

WICKES, Frances *The Inner World of Choice* (Coventure, London, 1977)
The Inner World of Childhood (Coventure, London, 1977)

YESUDIAN, Selvarajan *Yoga week by week* (Allen & Unwin, London, 1979)

ZUKAV, Gary *The Dancing Wu Li-Masters* (Rider, London, 1979)